# A HIDDEN PATH—

## Bethel Redding and Beyond

**A Sound Word Ministry
Publication**

ISBN #:978-1-64570-804-9

Authors: M. Barbara Hansell, Maria Chadim Kirkpatrick, Joy McCloud, and Oscar Whatmore

Contributors: Rick Becker, Bob Brunette

Special mention: Angie Deets, Tricia Pell

Special thanks for proofreading and editing: Robert H., Mary Lou Graeber

Front Cover photo by: Shutterstock – Bruce Rolff (Used by permission)
Back Cover photo by: Shutterstock -- Chinnapong (Used by permission)

Unless specified, "Scriptures taken from the NEW AMERICAN STANDARD BIBLE, Copyright 1960, 1962, 1963, 1968, 1971, 1975, 1977, 1995 by the Lockman Foundation. Used by permission."

All quotes have been left unedited, including spelling, grammar and punctuation.

Other booklets by Sound Word Ministry:
**Beware of the New Apostolic Reformation – English Version**
**Beware of the New Apostolic Reformation – Spanish Version**
**Narrow is the Way, Have You Really Found It?**
Available on Amazon and through our website—www.soundwordministry.org.

Authors can be reached at: soundwordministry1@gmail.com
**"Behold, I send you out as sheep in the midst of wolves; so be shrewd as serpents and innocent as doves." Matthew 10:16**

## DEDICATED—

To those whom the Lord has rescued and called out from the clutches of deception.

To those who love the flock enough to share the truth.

# Foreword

## Bob Brunette

I believe in present day American Evangelical Christianity (AEC), we are living in the midst of unparalleled measures of apostasy (/əˈpɒstəsi/; Greek: ἀποστασία apostasia) that are breaking out on every front imaginable. It is like what is described in the Book of Jeremiah—where a given society unleashed prophets, seemingly coming out of the woodwork at breakneck speed and in numbers never seen before. This phenomenon of false prophets, coupled with a great falling away, or turning aside by those once deemed to have been faithful followers of Christ is a condition which should bring all genuine followers of Christ to a strident position of "Attention"!

I believe one of the most treacherous groups of false prophets, purveyors of false gospel messages we see assailing the beloved body of Christ in our present day, is Bethel Church, Redding, CA—part of the New Apostolic Reformation (NAR) movement. The NAR movement is alternately known as Dominion Theology—a tainted, false apostolic/prophetic movement that actually leads genuine disciples of Christ astray into spiritual shipwreck.

I believe the authors at Sound Word Ministry have done an extraordinarily fine job at exposing the insidious deception and unbiblical nature of the NAR movement in their book, *A Hidden Path: Bethel Redding and Beyond*, to the ultimate end of drawing precious brothers and sisters back into the fold of Christ and away from spiritual destruction. I highly recommend its reading. (I John 2:18-19)

[Bob is the founder and facilitator of several international, apologetic, on-line watchdog groups that expose church deception.]


**NOTE: Some of the text in this book have video numbers next to them representing corresponding video numbers on our playlist. For added reference, you can view the videos by going to our website, soundwordministry.org, and then "Video Play Lists." You will find all the videos are listed there with the same number next to them that is listed next to the videos in this book.**

# Table of Contents

# I. Introduction to the New Apostolic Reformation (NAR)

*Christianity may well be facing the greatest challenge in its history: a series of powerful and growing seductions that are subtly changing biblical interpretations and undermining the faith of millions of people. Most Christians are scarcely aware of what is happening, and much less do they understand the issues involved...* [1]

Although false doctrines have invaded the Christian church since its inception, the above quote was written in 1985 long before the emergence of the New Apostolic Reformation (commonly referred to as NAR) or the other numerous, unbiblical beliefs and practices that have infiltrated the body of Christ today. But the largest threat to the Christian church currently is the New Apostolic Reformation.

The New Apostolic Reformation was founded and organized by C. Peter Wagner in 2001 and has been growing rapidly throughout the world ever since. The NAR is a highly deceptive movement of counterfeit spirituality—globally infiltrating biblical Christianity. It is made up of thousands of networks of churches and ministries that share core beliefs and a common agenda—to take dominion over the church and, subsequently, the world. One of its goals is to redefine Christianity as believers have known it for over 2000 years.

Their so-called "apostles" and "prophets" lead the movement professing extra-biblical, ongoing "new revelation" that they believe is needed to fulfill their God-given mandate—to establish a physical kingdom of God on earth. Christians need to realize that the NAR movement is part of a much bigger and more dangerous deception, especially because it has embraced practices and the teachings of the New Age movement. This is all done in the name of seeking more of the power of the "spirit" and the thirst for revival.

The leaders of the New Apostolic Reformation have cleverly stayed under the radar as many Christians have never heard of the movement. Even followers who engage in their practices are not aware of NAR's magnitude and the bigger picture of their agenda. Many pastors who are part of the NAR organization are not forthright (with their congregants) about their participation and, in some circles, even deny that NAR exists.

As you read this book, you will see how Gnosticism, the New Age and the Latter Rain have made their way into the teaching and activities of today's hyper-charismatic churches, all of which share similar agendas. We will present how leaders and teachers in the New Apostolic Reformation are using mysticism, the Kabbalah and other occult practices to further their mandate of dominionism. NAR is a worldly belief system masqueraded by Christian language and sprinkled with Christian doctrines. It is a mixture, and God hates a mixture!

Despite warnings by the early apostles throughout the New Testament about the importance of discernment and preserving sound doctrine, believers are deceived by the NAR teachers into thinking that they are to not judge or be negative towards things they have not seen or heard before, and are told that "God is doing a new thing." The Apostle Paul says otherwise:

> *Now I praise you because you remember me in everything and hold firmly to the traditions, just as I delivered them to you.* 1 Corinthians. 11:2

NAR advocates are replacing doctrine with experience. They are continuously leading conferences and selling books instructing unsuspecting believers to embrace extra-biblical knowledge in order to get closer to God even though these same practices are strictly forbidden in the Bible.

Gnostic beliefs are being accepted in the post-modern church— especially, for example, the belief that one can become enlightened by receiving keys to unlock hidden mysteries that God is suddenly revealing now. Along with Gnostics of the past, followers of the New Apostolic Reformation believe that they are an elite group that can achieve higher levels in Christ than those who are not followers of NAR. They teach that hidden knowledge is necessary in order to be ready to receive (a bigger and better) soon coming 2nd Pentecost. They receive this knowledge or gnosis by supernaturally communicating with the spirit realm—deceased, historical Bible figures and personal relatives, and through what they believe is direct revelation from God channeled through their "prophets."

8

Although sad, it is not surprising, because we are warned several times by Jesus in Matthew 24 when the disciples questioned Him about what would be the sign of His coming, and of the end of the age. His first response to the disciples' questions was to "see to it that no one misleads you," and that "many will come in My Name . . . and will mislead many." Paul tells us that a great apostasy (II Thessalonians 2:3) will happen before the return of Christ. This great apostasy will, of course, threaten all of Christendom.

## Catch phrases

In the New Apostolic Reformation, the following catch phrases and buzz words are spoken regularly to describe their activities—terms such as:

*accessing the gates of heaven, activation of the gifts, advancing the kingdom, alignment, angelic visitation, anointing, apostolic, appealing to heaven, ascending into new levels of glory, atmospheres, awakening the gifts, birthing, breakthrough, bringing heaven down to earth, changing the atmosphere, come up higher, contemplative prayer, covering, decreeing and declaring, dimensions, dreams, encounters, experiencing God, FIRE!, fire tunnels, for such a time as this, fresh revelation, fulfilling your destiny, getting drunk, glory carriers, glory clouds, God is doing a new thing, going deeper, going to another level, gold dust, healing rooms, hosting the presence, impartation, increase, intimacy with God (greater), Joel's Army, jumping in the river, legacy, levels of anointing, little gods, mandate, manifestations, mantles, marinating in the spirit, moving into your destiny, moving in the supernatural, mystical, new breed, new revelation, new sound, new wine, outpouring, paradigm shift, open heaven, open portals, prophetic words, rain, receive a double portion, receive a double anointing, releasing (whatever) into the atmosphere, restoration, revelation knowledge, seasons, secret place, Seven Mountain Mandate, shifting, slain in the spirit, soaking, spiritual mapping, staying in alignment, Strategic Level Spiritual Warfare, taking dominion, "the presence," third heaven, touch not God's anointed, transformation, transforming cities, transforming cultures, trances, trips to heaven, vibrations, visions, wind, world changers.*

If you are attending a church, and you are hearing words or phrases from the above list, you can be sure that your pastor or church is involved in some way or another. This book was written especially for you.

## Cult characteristics

Many believe that the New Apostolic Reformation is, in many ways, a cult—not only because of its false, extra-biblical doctrines and its elite group mentality (later explained in this book), but because of what one experiences when he or she chooses to leave.

Often when one begins to ask questions of pastors or leaders, he or she is treated hostilely, and spiritually and/or verbally abused. When one does choose to leave, it is also very common to experience many different kinds of emotional distresses on some level such as:

1.  **denial** that the NAR even exists
2.  **overwhelmed** about the vastness of the movement
3.  **confusion** about one's new understanding of God and the Bible contrary to what he or she was taught and believed while in the NAR—due to a sudden, radical change in theology
4.  **shock** at the realization of having been deceived
5.  **anger** at the deceivers, and at one's self because of the lack of discernment used regarding the huge mountain of deception he or she believed
6.  **fear** of being a part of another church and the thought of being deceived and mistreated again (many remain believers in Christ but never go back to an organized church)
7.  **loneliness and alienation** from friends, and relatives (including parents, children, and spouses left behind in the NAR)
8.  **depression** over shattered dreams and broken promises from "prophecies" that never materialized or were fulfilled
9.  **lost and detached** if and when one does decide to seek church fellowship—not knowing where they fit in or belong
10. **apathy**—especially difficulties being motivated to start and develop new relationships

Other emotions, that nearly all believers who leave the NAR experience, are the feelings of tremendous **loss** and deep **grieving** especially for their loved ones who are still left in the clutches of the delusion. In extreme cases, some even report having struggled with Post Traumatic Stress Disorder (PTSD). For many, the brokenness and emotions experienced above can take years to recover from. A resource for more detailed, actual testimonies of believers coming out of the NAR and what they experienced can be found in our booklet, *Narrow is the Way, Have You Really Found It?*

We are concerned that deception in the church continues to increase globally at an amazing speed. The subtle, disguised bait offered to undiscerning Christians is the oldest lie in the book—"you can be like God." Jude 23 tells us that we need to "save others, snatching them out of the fire; and on some have mercy with fear, hating even the garment polluted by the flesh."

This book is an attempt to do just that. It is our sincere desire not to be condemning but to bring a warning, and awareness as to what is happening in the body of Christ. One of the biggest and fastest growing venues of The New Apostolic Reformation is Bill Johnson and Bethel Church in Redding, California, which has had a tremendous effect on thousands of churches and millions of believers worldwide. It is truly **a hidden path** leading to destruction.

**Endnotes -- Introduction**
1.  Dave Hunt & T. A. McMahon, *The Seduction of Christianity*, Harvest House Publishers, Eugene, Oregon, 1985, p. 11]

## II. Brief History

Established in 1954, Bethel Church is a non-denominational, charismatic megachurch whose home base is in Redding, California. The church currently has 11,000 members, and is led by Bill and Beni Johnson. It is known for its controversial ministry style. Kris Vallotton serves as the Senior Associate Leader along with Johnson's sons, Brian and Eric, and several others on the leadership team as well.

Bethel Church is the home to: Bethel School of Supernatural Ministry (BSSM), Bethel School of Technology, Bethel Christian School (pre-K through 8th grade), Bethel Conservatory of the Arts, Worship U, Bethel TV, the music label—*Bethel Music* and the internationally known worship band—*Jesus Culture.*

The church actually began in 1952 with several families meeting in a private home. In 1954, it became an Assemblies of God church; and in

1968, Bill Johnson's father, Earl Johnson, became the pastor there. The current Pastor Bill Johnson was invited to lead the congregation in 1996. He gave only one stipulation before he was voted in—that the message would always be about revival, and that the subject of revival must never change. Bethel Church subsequently left the Assemblies of God denomination and became an independent church.

> *In 2005, the membership of Bethel Church voted unanimously to withdraw the church's affiliation with the Assemblies of God and became a non-denominational church. Johnson stated that the reason was—"not a reaction to conflict but a response to a call."[1]*

On the Bethel Church website, under the heading, "About," they describe themselves this way—

> *We are about REVIVAL . . . the personal, regional, and global expansion of God's Kingdom through His manifest presence.[2]*

What is the **manifest presence** mentioned in Bethel's mission statement? The word *manifest* means "readily perceived by the eye or understanding." This is different from God's omnipresence. The meaning of the word *omnipresence* is "present everywhere at the same time." God's presence is with us whether or not we see or feel Him. The manifest presence is a presence from God that we can see or feel.

Their description of who Bethel is continues on their website as follows:

> *. . .a congregation rooted in the love of God and dedicated to worldwide transformation through revival.[3]*

Although Bill Johnson denies his affiliation with the New Apostolic Reformation (NAR), the theology that he teaches and the practices demonstrated at Bethel Church line up with many NAR teachings and practices—along with a combination of the doctrines of Dominionism, Kingdom Now, the Seven Mountain Mandate, and the Word of Faith Movement.

### Endnotes – Brief History

1. https://en.wikipedia.org/wiki/Bethel_Church_(Redding,_California)
2. https://www.bethel.com/about/
3. Ibid.

# IV. False Doctrines

## Kenosis

In his book, *When Heaven Invades Earth*, Bill Johnson states very clearly that Jesus laid His divinity aside, and was a mere man in right relationship with God while doing his earthly ministry. Here are some quotes by Bill Johnson about who he believes Jesus is:

> *Jesus Christ said of Himself, "The Son can do nothing."... He had NO supernatural capabilities whatsoever! While He is 100 percent God, He chose to live with the same limitations that man would face once He was redeemed. He made that point over and over again. Jesus became the model for all who would embrace the invitation to invade the impossible in His name. He performed miracles, wonders, and signs, as a man in right relationship to God ... not as God. If He performed miracles because He was God, then they would be unattainable for us. But if He did them as a man, I am responsible to pursue His lifestyle. Recapturing this simple truth changes everything ... and makes possible a full restoration of the ministry of Jesus in His Church.* [1]

> *Jesus lived His earthly life with human limitations. He laid His divinity aside as He sought to fulfill the assignment given to Him by the Father: to live life as a man without sin, and then die in the place of mankind for sin* [2]

> *The outpouring of the Spirit also needed to happen to Jesus for Him to be fully qualified. This was His quest. **Receiving this anointing qualified Him to be called the Christ**, which means "anointed one." **Without the experience there could be no title**.* [3]
> [emphasis ours]

Simply put, the doctrine of *kenosis* is the belief that before Jesus was born and came to earth, He emptied Himself of deity and came as a man. He performed miracles as a man and **achieved** His deity and; therefore, we can also. This is a misinterpretation of Philippians 2. *Video #1* (@12:04-12:26). Kenosis deifies man while marginalizing the deity of Christ. It is also compatible with the beliefs that are taught in the New Age and in the Hindu religion—that the Christ consciousness can be achieved as one

13

reaches higher levels of enlightenment. In Greek, the word *kenoo* means emptying. However, it is important to understand that Jesus did not empty Himself of deity or exchange deity for humanity. In Philippians 2:7, the Bible says that "Jesus emptied Himself, taking the form of a bond-servant, and being made in the likeness of men." Jesus never stopped being God during His earthly ministry, but that He completely submitted Himself to the will of the Father.

On the website, *GotQuestions.org, kenosis* is further explained:

> . . . *We often focus too much on what Jesus gave up. The kenosis also deals with what Christ took on. Jesus added to Himself a human nature and humbled Himself. Jesus went from being the glory of glories in heaven to being a human being who was put to death on the cross. In the ultimate act of humility, the God of the universe became a human being and died for His creation. The kenosis, therefore, is Christ taking on a human nature with all of its limitations, except with no sin.* [4]

Johnson also twists John 5:19 as a way to support his beliefs as to how Jesus performed miracles and ministry:

> . . . *Many get hung up on the idea that Jesus did miracles as God, not man. In reality, as I said in my previous book, and I continue to remind people, Jesus had no ability to heal the sick. He couldn't cast out devils, and He had no ability to raise the dead. He said of Himself in John 5:19, the Son can do nothing of Himself." He had set aside His divinity. He did miracles as man in right relationship with God because He was setting forth a model for us, something for us to follow. If He did miracles as God, we would all be extremely impressed, but we would have no compulsion to emulate Him. But when we see that God has commissioned us to do what Jesus did – and more – then we realize that He put self-imposed restrictions on Himself to show us we could do it, too. Jesus so emptied Himself that He was incapable of doing what was required of Him by the Father – without the Father's help* [5]

John 5:19 does not suggest, in any way, Christ's inability or lack of deity. Jesus is talking about the intimacy and perfect oneness that he has with

His Father. Bob DeWaay says this about Jesus' deity on his online *Echo Zoe Ministries'* blog:

> *Deity cannot be gained, lost, laid down, or set aside. It either is or it isn't. Deity is defined as: non-contingent, external existence.*[6]

Johnson also takes the position of kenosis as a way to suggest that all Christians can achieve the same anointing that Jesus had. This belief and the doctrine of *kenosis* have been deemed heretical by the church for thousands of years. We are able to do the ministry of Christ—because He gives us the gifts and abilities to do so—not because of anything we can achieve or attain. God became human but never stopped being God.

In summary, Don Pirozok in his book, *Kingdom Come,* says this about *Kenosis:*

> *When a denial of Jesus Christ is preached like the heresy of kenosis to promote the availability of the "anointing for everyone," the foundation of Jesus Christ is corrupted. The preaching is not about the supremacy of Jesus Christ, or the emphasis of the cross, the confrontation of sin, the need for repentance, or preparation for the Second Coming of Jesus Christ. Instead, the church is being caught up into phenomena and experiences where the spirit of antichrist has substituted the authentic Jesus Christ for the "anointing." Only the anointing isn't pointing to Jesus Christ like the Holy Spirit is continually doing. The other "Christ" then becomes a man, a movement, a false doctrine, and false practice. Another Jesus preached with false doctrines, by a false gospel, seduced by manifestations of another spirit. All these warnings were given by the first century apostles. Why do we think modern NAR charismatic apostles and prophets are beyond this error?*[7]

Gnosticism was one of the heresies happening in the first century church. Wikipedia tells us more about what the Gnostics believed about the deity of Christ. [Wikipedia.org/wiki/Gnosticism].

> *Jesus is identified by some Gnostics as an embodiment of the supreme being who became incarnate to bring gnōsis to the earth, while others adamantly denied that the supreme being came in the*

15

*flesh, claiming Jesus to be merely a human who attained divinity through gnosis and taught his disciples to do the same.*

What we believe about the divinity of Jesus Christ differentiates Christianity from all other religions. It is the very core and essence of our faith. To say that Jesus "did miracles as man in right relationship with God because He was setting forth a model for us to follow" challenges and minimizes the divinity of Jesus and elevates us as human beings.

## On earth as it is in heaven

*The greatest mandate in this life is to pray "Your Kingdom Come, Your Will Be Done on earth as it is in Heaven[8]. —Bill Johnson*
***Video #1*** (@6:35-7:09)

The verse, "On earth as it is in heaven" has been adopted by Bethel Church, and the New Apostolic Reformation. In fact, it is the first thing one sees when visiting Bethel's website. It is at the crux of their doctrine and ministry ***Video #11*** (@14:30-15:17). They distort the phrase in the Lord's Prayer (Matthew 6:10) to mean that believers have the power and mandate from God to create an atmosphere to bring heaven down to earth. They believe that everything we expect to experience and see in heaven, we can experience and see on earth NOW. Here are a few more quotes by Bill Johnson on how important it is to him to pray heaven down to earth:

*If you want anything from God, you will have to pray into heaven. That is where it all is. If you live in the earth realm and expect to receive from God, you will never get anything.[9]*

*The Church has been negligent in one thing . . . she has not prayed the power of God out of heaven.[10]*

We are not instructed in the Bible to bring heaven down to earth or to pray the power of God out of heaven. It is not our mandate, and it is not even possible. The frightening thing is that the writings of Alice Bailey, a New Age practitioner, who channeled messages she received by a demonic spirit, agrees with Bill Johnson. Do Johnson and his followers know how much some of his teachings line up with the New Age? Probably not. We read the following from Alice Bailey:

16

*It is time that the church woke up to its mission which is to materialize the kingdom of God on earth today, here and now. The time is past wherein we emphasize a future and coming kingdom. People are no longer interested in a possible heavenly state or a probable hell. They need to realize that the kingdom is here and must express it on earth.* [11]

It is also taught at Bethel Church that signs and wonders, healings and miracles are evidence that heaven has been brought down to earth; not just because God, in His wonderful love and grace, bestows on His children—healing gifts and mercies. We, Christians, look forward to the day when there will be heaven on earth which can only happen when Jesus returns. Some final thoughts of Don Pirozok from his book, *Kingdom Come:*

*The heaven to earth message is related to an end-times view. Church is the Kingdom on earth and heaven is brought to the earth through the church. Instead of needing the physical return of Jesus Christ and the bodily resurrection of the saints, the church has already been vested with the power to transform the world. However, the world has never been, nor will ever be, converted by the church, nor does the church have the responsibility to bring the Kingdom of Heaven to earth; only God the Father and Jesus Christ the Son will execute the return of the Kingdom.* [12]

**Behold, the tabernacle of God is among men, and He will dwell among them, and they shall be His people, and God Himself will be among them, and He will wipe away every tear from their eyes; and there will no longer be any death; there will no longer be any mourning, or crying, or pain; the first things have passed away.** Revelation 20:3-4

## Health and Healing

Bill Johnson's beliefs on healing and prosperity are a combination of Word of Faith (WOF) teachings (which has its roots in New Thought, and the occult/New Age) mixed with Pentecostalism and the Bible. The Word of Faith Movement, whose tentacles are very far reaching, is a huge and exhaustive topic. It would take volumes to explain this movement in detail. This section is a brief account of what the Word of Faith is and how influential its teachings have been from its inception to the present.

You can trace the teachings of the Word of Faith back to a man named **Phineas Quimby** (1802-1866). He was the founder of New Thought (thought controls everything). Quimby used hypnosis as a way of healing. He taught that one has the power, by positive or negative thoughts, to control his or her life and future.

Phineas Quimby inspired many people including **Mary Baker Eddy** (founder of Christian Science), and **A. W. Kenyon** (known as the father of the Word of Faith movement). Kenyon also had tremendous influence on **Kenneth Hagin** who carried the Word of Faith movement into the modern church, to the point of even having been accused of plagiarizing Kenyon's writings. The Word of Faith influence can be seen in the teachings of many prosperity preachers in the church today, especially **Kenneth Copeland** who carried its beliefs even further, greatly increasing its popularity. You can see these preachers on television peddling their wares and convincing unsuspecting, needy believers that if you "sow a seed" by sending them (the ministers) money, you will then receive healing and/or a financial breakthrough from the Lord. The money preachers' message has always been the same—you can be rich, and you can be healed—NOW! In fact, you can have anything you want from God. New Thought was once considered extreme, but it has now become accepted in the modern church, especially in the Word of Faith, the NAR, and some inner healing circles.

**Faith is a force.** The Word of Faith followers believe that our faith is a force and our words and thoughts are carriers of that force. But do we have faith in God or faith in our faith and the force it carries? If we have faith in our own faith, then we don't have faith in God but faith in ourselves and our own force. In the book, *Seduction of Christianity*, Dave Hunt and T. A. McMahon say this:

> . . . *Such teaching has confused sincere Christians into imagining that "faith" is a force that makes things happen because they believe. Thus faith is not placed in God but is a power directed at God which forces Him to do for us what we have believed He will do. When Jesus said on several occasions, "Your faith has saved*

*[healed] you, He did not mean that there is some magic power triggered by believing, but that faith had opened the door for Him to heal them. If a person is healed merely because he believes he will be healed, then the power is in his mind, and God is merely a placebo to activate his belief. . . .That is the basic idea behind sorcery.* [13]

*If we can make God or some cosmic force do our bidding by the thoughts we think or words we speak, then we have achieved the sorcerer's goal: We have become masters of our own fate and can make anything happen that we want to happen simply by believing that it will happen. The power is in our belief, and God Himself must do what we believe He will do, because whatever we believe must come to pass!* [14]

**Positive confession.** Positive confession theology means that Christians can cause to happen what they say with their words. This kind of thinking has also been nicknamed: "name it and claim it," "blab it and grab it," "confess it and possess it," and "believe it and receive it" theology.

Word of Faith followers believe in the "Law of Attraction." This means that if we think and/or speak positively about something, good things will come to us. On the other hand, if we think and/or speak negatively about something—we curse ourselves, and bad things will come to us.

Word of Faith followers believe that because God Almighty spoke the words, "Let there be light and there was light"—so they also have the same creative power. People in the occult also believe that they have the power with their words to speak things into existence.

The main Scripture that the Word of Faith people use to support their belief in the power of their words is Romans 4:17:

> *. . . even God, who gives life to the dead and calls into being that which does not exist.*

However, we learn from this Scripture that it was not Abraham who spoke his miracle into existence—but God! We are not little gods! This belief is an over-estimation of our authority, and a usurpation of God's majesty and sovereignty. Dave Hunt and T. A. McMahon continue:

*Confess your healing, confess your prosperity, confess your dominion over this earth, confess your divine right; command God to heal and bless! Such confession is not the repentance that qualifies for the forgiveness which God offers by virtue of the fact that Jesus Christ has paid the full penalty for our rebellion.*[15]

*Many Christians make God Himself subject to law without realizing that they have destroyed Him in the process; **for who needs God if everything happens according to laws that even God must obey.** This eliminates true miracles and turns prayer into a technique for releasing divine power by following certain principles, rather than submitting to God's will and trusting His wisdom, grace, and love.* [16] [emphasis ours]

Paul tells us that he knew in advance he was going to suffer affliction and that affliction did, indeed, take place. He does not indicate to us, in any way, that he had the power to use his words to prevent adversity from happening. He even tells the Thessalonians that they shouldn't be disturbed by the possibility of affliction, because he (Paul) was destined for it. The following Scripture is contrary to what is taught by Bill Johnson and others in the Word of Faith movement.

> *So that no one would be disturbed by these afflictions; for you yourselves know that we have been destined for this.*
>
> *For indeed when we were with you, we kept telling you in advance that we were going to suffer affliction; and so it came to pass, as you know.* I Thess. 3:3-4

Notice, too, that the afflictions that Paul endured had nothing to do with a lack of his faith. Another similar Scripture can be found in Acts 20:22 where Paul tells the Thessalonians that he knew that in every city—bonds and afflictions awaited him. Again, there is no indication that Paul tried to pray those things away by "Strategic Level Spiritual Warfare" (a common practice taught and used by the NAR believers—supposedly exorcising territorial spirits and powerful demons that allegedly rule over cities, regions, and geographical areas from the second heaven where NAR followers believe that Satan dwells).

*And now, behold, bound by the Spirit, I am on my way to Jerusalem, not knowing what will happen to me there, except that the Holy Spirit solemnly testifies to me in every city, saying that bonds and afflictions await me.* Acts 20:22

**Decreeing and Declaring.** Believers of the Word of Faith and the New Apostolic Reformation believe that all they have to do to get what they want is to attach the magic formula phrase, "**I decree and declare**" before a prayer, and God has to do it. They point to Old Testament Scriptures where decrees were made and they think that God is bound by their every wish. In some NAR circles, followers believe that they can petition the "courts of heaven" with their decrees that contain legal rights to get themselves answers to prayer. In fact, several books have been written to show you how to do it.

In the book, The Physics of Heaven, Ellyn Davis, (a woman closely tied to Bill Johnson and Bethel Church) states that she believes that God has given us the power to call things into existence:

> *It shouldn't be a stretch for us to believe that, as "observers" to whom Jesus gave all power in heaven and earth, we can through faith, intent, prayer, and declaration call things into existence. Jesus has given us the power through our faith and our intent, to "pop a qwiff" and bring things from the unseen world into the visible.* [17]

One of the main Scriptures the NAR teachers use for decreeing and declaring is Job 22:28:

> *You will also decree a thing, and it will be established for you; and light will shine on your ways.*

But these words were spoken by Eliphaz the Temanite, one of Job's friends—not God. Later in chapter 42 of Job—we learn that God is angry with Eliphaz when He says this:

> *My wrath is kindled against you and against your two friends, because you have not spoken of Me what is right as my servant Job has.* Job 42:7

21

Even if well intended, when we say "I decree and declare," it takes the focus off of Jesus and causes the focus to be on "I," or "me." When Jesus was asked how to pray, it is clear that He immediately turned His focus to "Our Father who art in heaven. Hallowed be Thy name, Thy kingdom come, Thy will be done." Prayer is about petitioning God and His will.

"Decree" is mentioned in the Bible over 400 times and "declare" is mentioned over 200 times. Two examples are in the following Scriptures—David describes declaring God's work, and then Paul tells about declaring the gospel. This is much different than the way the Word of Faith followers apply decreeing and declaring.

> *Then all men will fear,*
> *And they will <u>declare</u> the work of the Lord,*
> *And will consider what He has done.* Psalm 64:9

> *Moreover, brethren, I <u>declare</u> unto you the gospel*
> *which I preached unto you, which also ye have*
> *received, and wherein ye stand.* I Cor. 15:1 KJV

**Little gods**. The "little gods" theology is this: (1) Adam was created with equal divinity as God. (2) He lost his divinity through the Fall of Man. (3) Through the atonement of Jesus, God provided a way for man to obtain his divinity back. (4) God had faith in His faith when He spoke the words that created the universe. (5) Because God lives inside of us, we have that same power—therefore, we are "little gods."

Bill Johnson tells us the following about the possibilities of a believer:

> *For us to become all that God intended, we must remember that Jesus' life was a model of what mankind could become if it were in right relationship with the Father. Through the shedding of His blood, it would be possible for everyone who believed on His name to do as He did and become as He was. This meant then that every true believer would have access to the realm of life that Jesus lived in.* [18]

Rick Becker, of Famine in the Land Ministry, writes in his *Normalizing Mysticism* article:

*In other words, whatever miracles Jesus performed, we as his followers are able to emulate, and even supersede. It is this thought that has influenced the minds of Bethelites, and caused them to view themselves as "little gods," hoping to walk through walls, walk on water, and raise the dead—the Trinity has morphed into a quartet.* [19]

**Jesus is perfect theology.** Bill Johnson teaches that everything we say and do should be seen and heard in the life of Jesus during the three and a half years that He walked on the earth because He alone is "perfect theology." Yet Jesus tells us that the whole of Scripture testifies about Him:

> **You search the Scriptures because you think that in them you have eternal life; it is these that testify about Me.** John 5:39

"Jesus is perfect theology" is a distorted, and unbalanced version of Christianity because Johnson does not believe that people should ever be sick. He teaches that Jesus heals every time.

*I refuse to create a theology that allows for sickness. Paul refers to his thorn in the flesh which has been interpreted as disease allowed or brought on by God. That is a different gospel. Jesus didn't model it and He didn't teach it. You have a false gospel if you don't teach that Jesus heals every time – always intends healing every time.* [20]  *__Video #2__* (@4:21)

Johnson is referring to II Corinthians 12:4. When you read the verse, you get a different picture than what Johnson is teaching. Obviously God did not heal Paul even after he asked three times. Does Johnson believe that Paul preached "a different gospel?"

> **Because of the surpassing greatness of the revelations, for this reason, to keep me from exalting myself, there was given me a thorn in the flesh, a messenger of Satan to torment me—to keep me from exalting myself! Concerning this I implored the Lord three times that it might leave me. And He has said to me, "My grace is sufficient for you, for power is**

*perfected in weakness." Most gladly, therefore, I will rather boast about my weaknesses, so that the power of Christ may dwell in me.* Therefore *I am well content with weaknesses, with insults, with distresses, with persecutions, with difficulties, for Christ's sake; for when I am weak, then I am strong.* II Cor. 12:7-10

When you add the following verses in Galatians 4:12-14, we read that Paul does not preach that we should not allow for sickness in this life.

*I beg of you, brethren, become as I am, for I also have become as you are. You have done me no wrong; but you know that it was because of a bodily illness that I preached the gospel to you the first time; and that which was a trial to you in my bodily condition you did not despise or loathe, but you received me as an angel of God, as Christ Jesus Himself.* Gal.4:12-14

**Heretical doctrines of healing.** A common Scripture quoted by Word of Faith teachers is: "By His stripes, we ARE healed." They suggest that ALL sickness was already eliminated at the cross, it is our responsibility to just receive it; and it is only through our negative thoughts that the devil can inflict sickness and/or we stay sick. Many teach that **if we are sick, it is our fault;** and/or if we ask God to heal us and we remain sick, it is because we don't have enough faith, haven't done enough spiritual warfare, or haven't decreed and declared enough. The same applies to wealth and prosperity. But in the case of wealth and prosperity—it's because we haven't tithed enough!

Another thing to consider is that many believers try the formulas of the Word of Faith with much passion and zeal. When they don't receive healing, after a period of time, they become disillusioned with God.

As a leader of a local church, this writer personally witnessed a pastor revisit his Word of Faith theology, and started preaching its doctrines from the pulpit again. After the church moved to the inner-city, a surge of broken and abused new believers began attending. The bad news is that they were told by their pastor that whatever they wanted or needed—all they had to do was just to ask God, believe it, and they would receive it. It is sad to say that within six months, every one of those new

24

believers (about 43 precious people) left. Many of them told me later, "It didn't work for me—God must not love me like he does others." Those new believers needed to be discipled, loved, and ministered to—heart to heart. Instead they got religious formulas and unrealistic promises that normally don't work. They did not get the true gospel.

The message that one gets from the Word of Faith group is that **healing is simple**. They portray an unrealistic approach to prayer, teaching that anything you want, you can have if you have the right formula, and pray it in faith *Video #1* (@13:39 – 14:02). But the plain truth is that healing is not so simple. There is adversity, there is tragedy, there is sickness and suffering in this life—Jesus said that there would be.

Another unbalanced message of Bill Johnson is that the church needs signs, wonders and miracles in order for the church to grow so that the unsaved can come to Christ. However, the Bible does not mention one miracle that John the Baptist took part in. Yet he was a humble man with a powerful ministry who knew his place in the kingdom of God. The Bible tells us this in John 3:30-31:

> *He must increase but I must decrease. He who comes from above is above all, he who is of the earth is from the earth and speaks of the earth. He who comes from heaven is above all.*

Furthermore, on the day of Pentecost, there are no miracles of healing recorded, and the church grew by 3000 converts in one day. In both instances, the message was clear:

> *Repent, and each of you be baptized in the Name of Jesus Christ for the forgiveness of your sins; and you will receive the gift of the Holy Spirit."* Acts 2:38

We realize that there are many sincere, unsuspecting believers in the Word of Faith and NAR movements. They seem to be unaware of the deception being taught and practiced in these groups and of its occult influences. Because the beliefs are taught in the Name of Jesus, the false teachings are easily overlooked by followers. Both movements have systematically perverted the very core of Christianity, and are presenting and demonstrating a different Christ and a counterfeit Christianity.

Although the teachings of the Word of Faith are not new, the way they are being marketed today is making them the most seductive and deceptive messages being preached since the beginning of the church.

We know that Christ healed every manner of sickness and disease—and that He still heals today. We also know that He told us that healing and deliverance would follow us believers. It is also true that we have power in His Name, and we need to passionately pray for the sick. But the Bible gives no formula for healing, makes no guarantees, nor mentions anything about positive confession, decreeing and declaring, or claiming a healing.

> *Therefore we do not lose heart, but though our outer man is decaying, yet our inner man is being renewed day by day. For momentary, light affliction is producing for us an eternal weight of glory far beyond all comparison.* II Cor. 4:16-17

Lastly, Paul tells Timothy to teach the things that Timothy has heard from him (Paul) and entrust them to faithful men who will be able to teach others also. Would Paul consider Bill Johnson, Kris Vallotton, Kenneth Copeland and myriads of others in the Word of Faith/New Apostolic Reformation faithful men?

> *The things which you have heard from me in the presence of many witnesses, entrust these to faithful men who will be able to teach others also. Suffer hardship with me, as a good soldier of Christ Jesus.* II Timothy 2:3

If the reader would like to learn more about the Word of Faith Movement, these three books are recommended reading:
*A Different Gospel*, by D. R. McConnell, Hendrickson Publishers
*The Seduction of Christianity* by Dave Hunt and T. A. McMahon, Harvest House
*The New Charismatics* by Michael G. Moriarty, Zondervan Publishing House

## Wealth and Prosperity

> *No one can serve two masters; for either he will hate the one and love the other, or he will be devoted to one and despise the other. You cannot serve God and wealth.* Matthew 6:24

> *For we never came with flattering speech, as you know, nor with a pretext for greed—God is witness.* I Thessalonians 2:5

*Do you know that God wants you to be wealthy? It may be contrary to what we're usually taught in the church, but I believe that wealth is a sign of God's blessing in your life, and it's how we are made to live as children of the living King! Think about it, if your Dad rules the world, then you are royalty on this earth and have access to everything He has access to." I want to make sure you're understanding that I'm not talking about being rich. Although fruit of a wealth mindset is living in abundance, wealth is much bigger than simply having a lot of money. Wealth is believing in the fullness of God's ability and desire to provide in your life . . .[21]—*Kris Vallotton

Vallotton's statement above presents a message and a different point of view than the Scriptures above it. In the Webster's Universal College Dictionary, the definition of greed is as follows: *excessive or rapacious desire, especially for wealth or possessions.*

In an effort to carry out the Dominion mandate, leaders of the New Apostolic Reformation believe that it is the responsibility of the church to completely eliminate systemic poverty. They believe that there will be no more poverty in the world when Christ returns. Not only that, but they teach that all Christians can be rich both financially, and prosper in every way—NOW! Many books are sold on the subject of wealth (One of Kris Vallotton's newer books is entitled, *Poverty, Riches and Wealth: Moving from a Life of Lack into True Kingdom Abundance*). Many formulas, and irresponsible promises are made every day and believed by gullible followers who want their financial dreams met. But what does the Bible say about being rich, and about being poor? The following are just a few of many verses:

## Being rich

*Now listen, you rich people, weep and wail because of the misery that is coming on you. Your wealth has rotted, and moths have eaten your clothes. Your gold and silver are corroded. Their corrosion will testify against you and eat your flesh like fire. You have hoarded wealth in the last days. Look! The wages you failed to pay the workers who mowed your fields are crying out against you. The cries of the harvesters have reached the ears of the Lord Almighty. You have lived on earth in luxury and self-indulgence. You have fattened yourselves in the day of slaughter.* James 5:1-6

*Do not lay up for yourselves treasures on earth, where moth and rust destroy and where thieves break in and steal, but lay up for yourselves treasures in heaven, where neither moth nor rust destroys and where thieves do not break in and steal. For where your treasure is, there your heart will be also.* Matt.6: 19-21

*But godliness with contentment is great gain, for we brought nothing into the world, and we cannot take anything out of the world. But if we have food and clothing, with these we will be content. But those who desire to be rich fall into temptation, into a snare, into many senseless and harmful desires that plunge people into ruin and destruction. For the love of money is a root of all kinds of evils. It is through this craving that some have wandered away from the faith and pierced themselves with many pangs.* 1 Timothy 6: 2b-10

*As for the rich in this present age, charge them not to be haughty, nor to set their hopes on the uncertainty of riches, but on God, who richly provides us with everything to enjoy. They are to do good, to be rich in good works, to be generous and ready to share, thus storing up treasure for themselves as a good foundation for the future, so that they may take hold of that which is truly life.* 1 Timothy 6: 17-19

Being poor:

> *They only asked us to remember the poor—the very thing I also was eager to do.* Galatians 2:10

> *Blessed are you who are poor, for yours is the kingdom of God.* Luke 6:20

> *For the poor you always have with you, and whenever you wish, you can do them good.* Mark 14:7

It is obvious from the above Scriptures, that a Christian is not promised a life of wealth and prosperity. In fact, we are warned many times that wealth is not to be our focus or even our goal. Again, the doctrine of prosperity originated in New Thought teachings. It trickled down through the years and infiltrated the church as a way to compete with the rise of materialism in the world.

To the contrary of what is promised by the Word of Faith/New Apostolic Reformation teachers, the health and wealth gospel is not what was modeled by Jesus and the early disciples, who certainly did not live a life of leisure, luxury, and financial prosperity. Leonard Ravenhill describes it this way: [goodreads.com]

> *The early church was married to poverty, prisons and persecutions.*

> *Today, the church is married to prosperity, personality and popularity.*

## Dominionism

A working definition of dominionism is the belief that God has given the church a mandate to build the kingdom of heaven on earth—restoring paradise by supernaturally taking control of all societal institutions. NAR Dominionists believe that it will be accomplished under the leadership of their "apostles" and "prophets" by subduing and ruling the earth—then and only then will Christ return. Their unusual interpretation of Genesis 1:26 is extreme because it includes the dominion of human beings who are not represented in the verse. Many who endorse the doctrine believe that after the church takes dominion, she will hand the nations over to Jesus. The popular mantra they use is that "Jesus will come **to** the church before He comes **for** the church."

The now deceased founder of the New Apostolic Reformation, C. Peter Wagner (chief "apostle" and friend to Bill Johnson), defined the dominion mandate this way—

> *A mandate means an authoritative order or command. It doesn't mean a good idea. It doesn't mean a suggestion. It means it is an authoritative order.*
>
> *Dominion has to do with control, has to do with leadership and subduing, and it relates to society.*[22] **\*Video #24\***

Wagner believed that taking dominion over the world is another way of saying "the Great Commission." He emphatically stated that God has given the church a mandate to take dominion over the earth and that includes people groups. He continues this way:

> *Jesus delegated—establishing His kingdom to us. We are the ones who are supposed to bring this about.*[23] **\*Video #24\***

In the book, *Vengeance is ours: The Church in Dominion*, Al Dager lists two other definitions of Dominionism:

> *A basic premise of dominion theology is that when Adam sinned, not only did man lose dominion over the earth, but God also lost control of the earth to Satan. Since that time, some say, God has been on the outside looking in, searching for a "covenant people" who will be His "extension" or "expression" in the earth to take dominion back from Satan. According to the dominionist interpretation, this is the meaning of the Great Commission.*
>
> *Some teach that this is to be accomplished through certain "overcomers" who, by yielding themselves to the authority of latter-day apostles and prophets, will take control of the kingdoms of this world. These kingdoms are defined as the various social institutions, such as the "kingdom" of education, the "kingdom"*

*of science, the "kingdom" of the arts, and so on. Most especially there is the "kingdom" of politics and government.* [24]

*Dominion theology is predicated upon three basic beliefs: (1) Satan usurped man's dominion over the earth through the temptation of Adam and Eve; (2) The Church is God's instrument to take dominion back from Satan; (3) Jesus cannot or will not return until the Church has taken dominion by gaining control of the earth's government and social institutions.* [25]

Dominionists believe that God has revealed to them the strategy of the Seven Mountain Mandate as a way to penetrate, influence and dominate the institutions of —(1) family, (2) government, (3) education, (4) arts/entertainment, (5) media, (6) business, and (7) religion. The Seven Mountain Mandate is a means to achieve their dominion goals because they believe that if they take control of these seven areas of life, they will be able to rule the nations. They also believe that when the church sets up the kingdom here on earth—Jesus can return. They believe that He cannot and will not return until the church fulfills the dominion mandate that they naively think was given to them by God.

Many dominionists are preterists or partial preterists. A preterist believes that the tribulation already happened in 70 A.D. even though most scholars agree that the Book of Revelation was not written until approximately 90 A.D. The preterist viewpoint is necessary as a dominionist because they also believe that the world is going to keep getting better and better, because the church is going to transform and take dominion over it. Many preterists also deny any future prophetic plans for the nation of Israel. In the book, *Dominion*, C. Peter Wagner revealed his views on preterism and his dominionist agenda:

*. . . But none of the signs of Matthew 24:4-34 are expected to precede His return, because they have already occurred.* [26] [C. Peter Wagner admitted in his book that he is a preterist.]

*We no longer accept the idea that society will get worse and worse because we now believe that God's mandate is to transform society so that it gets better and better.* [27] [Scripture clearly teaches that this world will continue to get worse as we move into the last days.

In fact, Jesus tells us that events getting worse is a very sign that he's coming back soon—and that we should "look up," not take over!]

Kris Vallotton, on his online blog of November 11, 2015, also outlines preteristic viewpoints with his eight eschatological core values listed below. It is apparent that these core values line up with the New Apostolic Reformation/Dominionist/Kingdom Now teachings. Vallotton does not give any Scriptures to back up his statements. We can understand because they are not biblical. We have ascribed a Scripture under each one of Vallotton's core values to reflect the contrast between truth and error.

1. *I will not embrace an end-time worldview that re-empowers a disempowered devil.*
[*It was also given to him to make war with the saints and to overcome them.*]
Rev. 13:7

2. *I will not accept an eschatology that takes away my children's future, and creates mindsets that undermine the mentality of leaving a legacy.*
[*To obtain an inheritance which is imperishable and undefiled and will not fade away, reserved in heaven for you.*] I Peter 1:4

3. *I will not tolerate any theology that sabotages the clear command of Jesus to make disciples of all nations and the Lord's Prayer that earth would be like heaven.*
[*There will be signs in the sun and moon and stars, and on the earth dismay among nations, in perplexity at the roaring of the sea and the waves, men fainting from fear and the expectation of the things which are coming upon the world; for the powers of the heavens will be shaken. Then they will see the SON of MAN COMING IN A CLOUD with power and great glory. But when these things begin to take place, straighten up and lift up your heads, because your redemption is drawing near.*] Luke 21:25-28

4. *I will not allow any interpretation of the Scriptures that destroys hope for the nations and undermines our command to restore ruined cities.*
[*And the light of a lamp will not shine in you any longer; and the voice of the bridegroom and bride will not be heard in you any longer; for your merchants*

*were the real men of the earth, because all the nations were deceived by your sorcery.]* Revelation 18:1-2, 23

5. *I will not embrace an eschatology that changes the nature of a good God.*

*[. . . Fall on us and hide us from the presence of Him who sits on the throne, and from the wrath of the Lamb; for the great day of their wrath has come, and who is able to stand?]* Rev. 6:16-17

6. *I refuse to embrace any mindset that celebrates bad news as a sign of the times and a necessary requirement for the return of Jesus.*

*[But when these things begin to take place, straighten up and lift up your heads, because your redemption is drawing near.]* Luke 21:28

7. *I am opposed to any doctrinal position that pushes the promises of God into a time zone that can't be obtained in my generation and, therefore, takes away any responsibility I have to believe God for them in my lifetime.*

*[For I consider that the sufferings of this present time are not worthy to be compared with the glory that is to be revealed in us.]* Roman 8:18

8. *I don't believe that the last days are a time of judgment, nor do I believe God gave the church the right to call for wrath for sinful cities. There is a day of judgment in which GOD will judge man, not us.* [28]

*[When the Lamb broke the fifth seal, I saw under the altar the souls of those who had been slain because of the word of God, and because of the testimony which they had maintained; and they cried with a loud voice, saying: 'How long, O Lord, holy and true, will You refrain from judging and avenging our blood on those who dwell on the earth?]* Revelation 6:9-10

Kris Vallotton also quotes Bill Johnson posted on his website [www.krisvallotton.com]:

*God is in charge but
He is not in control.
He has left us in control.*[29]
***Video#2*** @:09-3:17

33

Praise the Lord that He has never left us in control and never will. In fact, it gives us much peace, as a Christian, to know that God, indeed, is fully in control! Instead of the focus being on the blessed hope for the return of Jesus Christ to rescue His church (which was the belief that was shared by the apostles and Christians throughout the centuries)—rather the focus of the New Apostolic Reformation has shifted to the glorification of the church to redeem society. Jesus didn't come as a military leader or government bureaucrat—He came to change people's hearts, forgive sin and give us eternal life.

> **And the seventh angel sounded; and there were great voices in heaven, saying, The kingdoms of this world are become the kingdoms of our Lord, and of his Christ; and he shall reign for ever and ever.** Rev. 11:15

## Jesus was born again.

Bill Johnson teaches that Jesus was born the first time through the Virgin Mary, but because He ceased to be God and became sin, He had to be born again in the resurrection. He had to get saved!

> *Did you know that Jesus was born again? I asked the first service and they said, "No." But I will show it. It's in the Bible. He had to be. He became sin.* [30] *Video #3*

This teaching is not new. A similar one was taught by the father of the Word of Faith movement, A. W. Kenyon, that Jesus needed to be born again.

> *Kenyon taught that Jesus Christ was imputed with Satan's nature on the cross, died spiritually, and went to hell to suffer in our place. Since sin and sickness are purely spiritual, according to Kenyon, mere physical death could never atone, nor could it deal with the source of sin and sickness: Satan.* [31]

In summary, Jesus Christ did not have a sinful nature. He did not need to be born again. Bob DeWaay shares the following about the divinity of Christ:

34

*A heretical view of Jesus is taught that says He laid aside His divinity while on earth. This is heresy because divinity, by definition, is not a quality that can be laid aside. **If there was a time that Jesus was not divine, He was never divine to begin with, nor ever will be.**[32]* [emphasis ours]

## New Revelation vs. Sola Scriptura

*No one in their right mind would claim to understand all that is contained in the Bible for us today. Yet to suggest that more is coming causes many to fear. Get over it, so you don't miss it.*— Bill Johnson[33]

> **O Timothy, guard what has been entrusted to you, avoiding worldly and empty chatter and the opposing arguments of what is falsely called "knowledge"— which some have professed and thus gone astray from the faith. Grace be with you.** I Timothy 6:20-21

Knowledge and hidden mysteries are extremely important to Bill Johnson. Although he does teach about the importance of reading the Bible, he teaches a double message; in that, he also intensely emphasizes the need for experiencing God through extra-biblical information also known as "revelation knowledge." Remember it is part of Bethel's mission statement— "the personal, regional, and global expansion of God's kingdom through His manifest presence." In fact, hearing God speak "prophetically" on a daily basis is a common practice at Bethel Church.

There are many ways that one can "experience God" at Bethel. Some examples are: contemplative prayer/meditation, out-of-body trips to heaven, receiving messages from angels and departed saints, prophetic words, open visions, dreams, and trances, just to name a few. Of course, listening for God's voice is not, in itself, a false practice—unless what one hears is new and different from what is found in the Bible. Paul cautions us in Galatians 1:8:

*But even if we, or an angel from heaven, should preach to you a gospel contrary to what we have preached to you, he is to be accursed.*

The venues used by Johnson and the believers of the New Apostolic Reformation are dangerous because many of them listed require altered states of consciousness of some sort, and they leave one vulnerable to a false spirit, a false Jesus, and/or false doctrines. This is especially true because much of what is being channeled through participants of these practices ARE different than what Paul preached and what can be found in the entire New Testament.

*But I am afraid that, as the serpent deceived Eve by his craftiness, your minds will be led astray from the simplicity and purity of devotion to Christ. For if one comes and preaches another Jesus whom we have not preached, or you receive a different spirit which you have not received, or a different gospel which you have not accepted, you bear this beautifully.* II Corinthians 11:3-5

Johnson has his followers believing that they cannot live a "normal" Christian life without receiving regular revelation from God.

*It is absolutely impossible to live the normal Christian life without receiving regular revelation from God.*[34]

Johnson also tells his followers that they need to "be willing to go off the map, to go beyond what they know"—which essentially means to turn off their brains and let the "spirit" take over. In light of the fact that the Bible continuously cautions us to test every spirit, and that, if possible, even the elect will be deceived—this is another very dangerous teaching!

*. . .Those who feel safe because of their intellectual grasp of Scriptures enjoy a false sense of security. None of us has a full grasp of Scripture, but we all have the Holy Spirit. He is our common denominator who will always lead us into truth. But to follow Him, we must be willing to follow off the map—to go beyond what we know. To do so successfully we must recognize His presence above all.*[35]

Instead of teaching his followers to discern and test the spirits with the Word of God, Johnson instructs his followers as to how they can truly know when God is speaking. His method is not found anywhere in the Bible and continues to mislead people, very quickly, into deception.

*You'll know when He is speaking because it will have a freshness to it. It will always be better than anything you could have thought up yourself. And if He gives you new ideas, they will probably be impossible for you to accomplish in your own strength. His thoughts will so overwhelm you that you'll want to draw close to him so they can be accomplished.*[36]

Johnson also teaches that revelation knowledge releases power from heaven that will change the way we live.

*The Spirit of revelation opens up our knowledge of who God is, and from that comes the release of power from heaven. That power gives us access to all things pertaining to life and godliness. That encounter with God will not only shape the world around you, it will shape the world through you.*[37]

But Johnson even goes to the extreme to say that we will perish without prophetic revelation.

*We thrive with prophetic revelation, but perish without it.*[38]

The following is more of a sampling of quotes on the subject of extra-biblical revelation vs. *Sola Scriptura* (Scripture alone) taken from Johnson's many writings:

*We've gone as far as we can with our present understanding of Scripture. It's time to let signs have their place.*[39]

*We can and must know the God of the Bible by experience.*[40]

*Any revelation from God's Word that does not lead us to an encounter with God only serves to make us more religious. The Church cannot afford "form without power," for it creates Christians without purpose.*[41]

*Many hide their need to be in control behind the banner of "staying anchored to the Word of God."* [42]

*The pride that comes from mere Bible knowledge is divisive. It creates an appetite for one's own opinion.* [43]

Yet the Bible says:

> **All Scripture is inspired by God and profitable for teaching, for reproof, for correction, for training in righteousness;**
>
> **So that the man of God may be adequate, equipped for every good work.** *2 Timothy 3:16-17*

The Greek word for **equipped** is *exartizo* (Strong's #1822 biblehub.com). It means complete, finished, perfect, accomplished, or supplied. We are told that we don't need to look elsewhere. In fact, Paul tells us in Colossians 1:25-28 what the true hidden mysteries are:

> **Of this church I was made a minister according to the stewardship from God bestowed on me for your benefit, so that I might fully carry out the preaching of the word of God, that is, the mystery which has been hidden from the past ages and generations, but has now been manifested to His saints, to whom God willed to make known what is the riches of the glory of this mystery among the Gentiles, which is Christ in you, the hope of glory. We proclaim Him, admonishing every man and teaching every man with all wisdom, so that we may present every man complete in Christ.**

This is opposite of what Johnson tells his followers—that 2000 years of our Christian roots are insufficient, and that God's full intention for His people are reserved for His people now (the elite group of believers). It's like a perpetual carrot that he and other leaders of the NAR dangle in front of the noses of thousands of unsuspecting and undiscerning sheep, promising them that God is ready to reveal the newest revelation, mystery, anointing, outpouring, or breakthrough.

*I'm convinced that the pace of revelation will increase very rapidly in these last hours of history... That acceleration of revelation is beginning in our day ... It's about the purposes of God being unveiled on the planet. On-going revelation and encounters with the power of God launch us into understanding of things we've never understood before.* [44]

Johnson continuously makes the distinction between the following half-truths and the Bible as to the necessity to hear the voice of the Holy Spirit.

*Jesus did not say, "My sheep will know my book." It is His voice that we are to know. Why the distinction? Because anyone can know the Bible as a book—the devil himself knows and quotes the Scriptures. But only those whose lives are dependent on the person of the Holy Spirit will consistently recognize His voice.* [45]

The need for more revelation contained in the NAR belief system diminishes the power and truth of the Scriptures in favor of a personal encounter—assumed to be the true Holy Spirit. Assumption is especially dangerous in light of the fact that nearly all cults and false religions were founded upon the premise that some angel or voice spoke to a willing participant who received a "new doctrine" or "new revelation," and then started a new religion or movement.

### Experiencing God vs. the Word of God

Kris Vallotton, Senior Associate Leader at Bethel also has strong beliefs about the importance of experiencing God and voices them on his Facebook page dated 7/15/13:

*We are Christ to the world. I don't mean that we just preach Christ to the world. I mean that people should experience Christ when they meet us because it is Jesus who is being formed in us. As a matter of fact, it is no longer I who live, but Christ who lives in me.*

Yes, it is true that Jesus is being formed in us, and it is no longer we who live, but Christ who lives in us. However, Vallotton continues:

*When people experience us preaching the Word without us becoming the Word, the gospel gets reduced to a mere*

39

*philosophy—principles to be argued and words that can be wrangled over.* **But when the Word becomes flesh and dwells among us,** *they find themselves pierced to the heart and convicted in the depths of their very souls. It is incumbent upon us as the people of God to preach Christ wherever we go and, if necessary, use words!* [emphasis ours]

The Word became flesh—once. The Word is Jesus Christ. Anything else adds to the following Scriptures and are utter distortions:

> **In the beginning was the Word, and the Word was with God, and the Word was God. He was in the beginning with God. All things came into being through Him, and apart from Him nothing came into being that has come into being.** John 1:1-3

> **And the Word became flesh, and dwelt among us, and we saw His glory, glory as of the only begotten from the Father, full of grace and truth.** John 1:14

Furthermore, as we read Vallotton's statement above, we are led to ask the following questions:

1. Is it possible that the Word of God can **ever be reduced** to anything, let alone a "mere philosophy—principles to be argued and words that can be wrangled over" as Vallotton claims?

> **For I am not ashamed of the gospel, for it is the power of God for salvation to everyone who believes.** Romans 1:16

The above verse (Romans 1:16) actually contradicts so much of what Bethel is about! In their assertions (and the whole premise of much of what they teach) they minimize the power of the gospel which, in turn, explains their idolatrous obsession with "encounters" and "the presence," which they talk about as a thing in its own right.

> **For the word of the cross is foolishness to those who are perishing, but to us who are being saved it is the power of God.** I Corinthians 1:18

2. Is there anything at all that we can do or show people that "pierces their hearts or convicts them in the depths of their very souls" as Vallotton shares—other than the Bible?

> *For the word of God is living and active and sharper than any two-edged sword, and piercing as far as the division of soul and spirit, of both joints and marrow, and able to judge the thoughts and intentions of the heart.* Hebrews 4:12

3. Is Vallotton's statement another attempt to subtly or not so subtly declare that we are little gods?

> *Therefore God also has highly exalted Him and given Him the name which is above every name, that at the name of Jesus every knee should bow, of those in heaven, and of those on earth, and of those under the earth, and that every tongue should confess that Jesus Christ is Lord, to the glory of God the Father.* Philippians 2:5

4. Are these words by Kris Vallotton another way to lead his followers to believe that the Bible and preaching the gospel is not enough but that God depends on us to demonstrate signs and wonders in order for people to get saved? There is only one Great Commission given to us by our Lord:

> *Go into all the world and <u>preach the gospel</u> to all creation. He who has believed and has been baptized shall be saved; but he who has disbelieved shall be condemned.* Mark 16:15-16

Jesus goes on to tell us in the next two verses that signs and wonders will **follow** those who believe. He does not tell us that miracles are necessary in order for one to believe. It's the Holy Spirit that draws one to repentance and salvation. Again, they take the focus off of God and put it on man.

> *Faith cometh by hearing and hearing by the word of God.* Romans 10:17

## The "presence" vs. the Word of God

In addition to the importance of receiving extra-Biblical revelation, Bill Johnson expresses his strong views on experiencing "the presence" vs. the Word of God. In an online video, Johnson says this:

> *There is a dramatic increase in 'the presence.'* *He is wanting to raise up a generation of people that will learn to live from "the presence" of God as opposed to merely living from the principles of God, and that is a big deal. Because with the principles, there is success; but with "the presence," there is no failure. And that's what the Lord is looking for. A company of people who will carry His "presence" because then we impact every room we walk into, impact every group that we talk to.* ***Because words become spirit the way Jesus taught in John 6.*** *We change the atmosphere of cities.* [45a] ***Video #11*** (@13:21-14:12) [emphasis ours]

What Johnson says in the above quote is double speak—a twist of words. Is this yet another example of how he subtly teaches that experiencing "the presence" bears more fruit than "merely" believing in The Bible ("principles")? If so, this minimizes the power of the Word of God.

> ***It is the Spirit who gives life; the flesh profits nothing; the words that I have spoken to you are spirit and are life.*** John 6:63

Another vague choice of words is when Johnson states that "words become spirit the way Jesus taught in John 6." We sincerely hope that he believes that it is the words of Jesus and not ours that bring life. It is especially unclear coming from a leader who is part of a movement that teaches that we are "little gods," and that our words have creative power.

Jesus is the Word and is the Life—and not our words because of a special "anointing" or divine "presence" that we carry. Does Jesus even make the slightest implication that it is OUR words that become spirit and life the way His does, or that we can change the atmosphere of cities? In comparison, Jesus instructed his disciples, when they were not received, they were to shake the dust off their feet and move on.

Here is John 6:63 from the Amplified Bible:

*It is the Spirit Who gives Life [He is the Life-giver]; the flesh conveys no benefit whatever [there is no profit in it]. The words (truths) that I have been speaking to you are spirit and life.*

The Word of Life is empowered by the Holy Spirit to raise dead people (unregenerate, dead in trespasses and sin) to life. This is the domain of God—NOT OURS! Rick Becker, in the Famine in the Land Ministry online article, *Normalizing Mysticism* says this:

> *Believers who hunger and thirst after righteousness will be filled, not by experiences, but by abiding in Christ and his Word. The Holy Spirit illuminates the Word of God to us, and leads us into the discovery of truth that is objective and complete. The "more" sought by Johnson and his underlings is a never ending quest that will entertain their senses and cause them to be mesmerized by the angel of light.*[46]

Becker continues in the same article:

> *Bethel is not revealing new truth or accessing unique gifts, they are simply promulgating old heresies and delving in either vain imaginations or the occult. A real apostle – Paul, warned that mysticism and Gnosticism have no place in the church. Wisdom and knowledge can be found in Christ, not in supernatural God experiences or special knowledge given to the "uniquely gifted." God has revealed himself in and through Christ, with the purpose of giving us understanding; understanding that helps us discern between truth and error. God gives us full assurance and understanding and knowledge of God's mystery.*[47]

Paul tells us in the Book of Colossians that the mystery is Christ:

> *For I want you to know how great a struggle I have on your behalf and for those who are at Laodicea, and for all those who have not personally seen my face, that their hearts may be encouraged, having been knit together in love, and attaining to all the wealth that comes from the full assurance of understanding, resulting in a true knowledge of God's*

*mystery, that is, Christ Himself, in whom are hidden all the treasures of wisdom and knowledge. I say this so that no one will delude you with persuasive argument.* Colossians 2:1-4

Although we are not cessationists (Christians who believe that the gifts of the Spirit have ceased, and that God only speaks via the Bible), we believe that *Sola Scriptura* ("Scripture alone") is the absolute source for all doctrine and practice (principles and morals) now and forever. We do not believe that God is giving "new revelation" to the present day church so that believers can get to the next level, or keep abreast of the new things He is doing or is vital to the Christian walk. Furthermore, we do not believe that God forgot to tell us something in the Bible that He suddenly wants to reveal now.

We do believe that the gifts of the Spirit are still active today, however, they are tremendously misused and abused by people in the NAR churches. Lastly, we believe that there is a big difference between charismatic and "charismania," or as some describe what is happening in a segment of the church today—"NARismania."

## Manifestation of the Sons of God (MSOG)

One of the most radical heresies in the hyper-charismatic church and the New Apostolic Reformation is the doctrine of the Manifestation of the Sons of God (MSOG). This is not a new teaching at all but a common theme among cults and various fringe groups throughout the centuries. One of the beliefs of the Manifestation of the Sons of God doctrine is that there will be an elite, end-times remnant "super church" that will transform the world and bring heaven to earth. They also believe that the church will usher in a huge revival of a billion souls before the Second Coming of Jesus Christ.

### New Order of the Latter Rain
The Manifested Sons of God is a belief system that was adopted by the New Order of the Latter Rain (NOLR), also known as Latter Rain, which was a movement that was popular during the 1940's. The movement was dismantled mostly because of the strong stand taken by the leadership of the Assemblies of God denomination who renounced the Latter Rain

doctrines as heresy at that time. But during the 1990's, the agenda of the NOLR revisited the church once again but with another name—The New Apostolic Reformation (NAR). Much of what is taught today in the NAR churches is similar, if not the same, as the beliefs and practices found in the Latter Rain movement of the past.

Michael Moriarty in his book, *The New Charismatics*, explains about the roots of the Manifestation of the Sons of God heresy and how it affects the church today:

> *The Manifested Sons of God as a movement disbanded as a result of many scandals, doctrinal excesses, power abuses, and bizarre practices, which earned them a cult-like treatment in the headlines of orthodox Christianity. Nevertheless, many followers have carried their ideas to other churches who are similar in orientation, just not as extreme. The dissipation of the Manifested Sons did not result in an abolition of their teachings, only in a transference of them. Manifested Sons of God devotees have quietly entered various charismatic churches throughout the world, and their teachings have found fertile soil, eagerly germinating.*[48]

## Second Pentecost
In order to fulfill their dominionist aspirations of taking over the world, proponents of the Manifestation of the Sons of God doctrine prophesy that there will be a second Pentecost when God will manifest Himself through a select, elite, many-membered remnant body which will give them more supernatural power than the believers experienced in the early church.

## Immortalization
Some also believe that they will continue to receive more and more of God's power until they become "manifest" as sons of God—one in nature and in essence with Christ—so much so that they will have the ability to defeat death itself BEFORE the return of Christ. From Wikipedia, we learn about the supernatural power that dominionists believe they will attain:

> *A major feature of the expected latter rain would be the "manifestation of the Sons of God" or "Joel's Army". The Latter*

Rain movement taught that as the end of the age approached, the *"overcomers"* would arise within the Church. *Various branches debated the nature and extent of this manifestation. These Manifest Sons of God, ones who have come into the full stature of Jesus Christ, would receive the Spirit without measure. They would be as Jesus was when he was on earth and would receive a number of divine gifts, including the ability to change their physical location, to speak any language through the Holy Spirit, and would be able to perform divine healings and other miracles. They would complete the work of God, restoring man's rightful position as was originally mandated in Genesis. By coming into the full stature of Christ, they would usher in his millennial reign.* [49]

## An Elite Group

Bill Johnson tells us what he believes about this special, elite anointing:

> *He [the Holy Spirit] lives in all believers, but the glory of His presence comes to rest on only a few.* [50]

NAR leaders teach that there will be an army of believers called "Joel's Army," also known as the "Elijah Generation," or the "Elijah Revolution." They teach that a remnant of the church (a new breed) is the army that is referred to in Joel 2 when, in fact, the Bible describes there, a demonic, hostile army of locusts (also mentioned in Revelation 9:7-11). There is nothing in Joel 2 that suggests that what is being described is an army of elite, end-times Christians. Bill Johnson continues:

> *We will carry the Elijah anointing in preparing for the return of the Lord. In the same way that John the Baptist carried the Elijah anointing and prepared the people for the coming of the Lord.* [51]

NAR speaker and author, Johnny Enlow in his book, *The Seven Mountain Prophecy*, describes what the Elijah anointing will do (before Christ returns). Please notice who is doing the destroying. One has to ask if this is based on truth—or is it delusion? Unfortunately, many agree with his mentality!

46

*Elijah will first come and raise up that which will destroy the spirit of Baal and the spirit of Jezebel here on earth.* **We** *are going to take on the false prophet and the beast, and* **we're** *going to annihilate both of them. When they are crushed,* **we** *will come to the Lord and say, "The kingdoms of this world have become the kingdoms of our God" (Rev. 11:15).* **We will present the nations of the world to the Lord** *as His possessions.* **They** *will be the dowry that the Father is providing for* **us** *to present to the Bridegroom. Lovesick for His bride, Jesus will no longer be able to restrain Himself and will burst through the clouds to come sweep us off our feet. Our Prince Charming will come on a white horse to take us away. (See Revelation 19:11). But He's not coming for a lazy, spoiled prostitute—He's coming for an overcoming, conquering, love-motivated bride who has made herself ready by fulfilling her mission. (See Revelation 19:7.) The Elijah Revolution is the catalyst for all of these things.*[52] [emphasis ours]

## Little gods

Another part of the Manifestation of the Sons of God doctrine is that humanity can become divine. Michael Moriarity explains:

*They [referring to the New Order of the Latter Rain] taught that a human being can become God, that a person can become perfect, and that he or she can become Christ . . . Those who reach this glorified state are worthy to judge the ungodly world and rule in the kingdom of God.*[53]

Michael Moriarty continues to explain more about what is believed will happen to this elite group:

*The second coming of Christ has two phases: the literal and the spiritual. In the spiritual phase, Christ would manifest himself through this many-membered body—the overcomers preparing for "manifestation." In the second phase, Christ would manifest himself in a spiritual visitation to his elect and would later personally return to a glorious kingdom on earth, ushered in by his perfect, incorruptible church. The more militant Manifested Sons totally spiritualized the one in nature and in essence. Being*

47

*one with Christ corporately resulted in a body of "little Christs" manifesting Jesus Christ on earth as his ongoing incarnation.* [54]

## Spirit of Sonship/Adoption

In the online article, *Bethel Church Peddling New Breed Heresy, Part I: Spirit of Sonship = Spirit of Adoption* [posted on 5/28/17 by ChurchWatcher], the best description is presented about the Manifestation of the Sons of God doctrine and how the NAR believes they can become one with Christ or "little gods."

| | | |
|---|---|---|
| 1. | **Kenosis** – Jesus empties Himself of deity | **Spirit of Adoption** – we imitate Kenosis Jesus |
| 2. | **Alignment** | We and Jesus align with the Father. |
| 3. | **Ascension** | We and Christ have ascended and are seated on the right hand of the Father |
| 4. | **Glorification** | We and Christ are to manifest Father's glory here on earth as gods.[55] |

The *Churchwatcher* article goes on to show how the NAR distorts the passages in Romans 8. It describes the connection between Romans 8:15 (spirit of adoption) and Romans 8:19 (sons of God) related to the information above. We suggest that you read the entire excellent article [address found in the endnotes.]

> *For you have not received a spirit of slavery leading to fear again, but you have received a spirit of adoption as sons by which we cry out, "Abba! Father!"* Rom. 8:15

> *For the anxious longing of the creation waits eagerly for the revealing of the sons of God.* Rom. 8:19

Bill Johnson in his online video, *Thinking from the Throne,* shares what he believes regarding the resurrection and who we are in Christ:

*Jesus was raised from the dead by the* **spirit of resurrection***. He was ascended to heaven and was seated at the right hand of the Father and then was glorified.* **So we have resurrected, ascended and glorified.** *[*emphasis ours*]*

*Jesus accomplished that on your behalf and mine. So much so that the Bible says that we were raised with Him. So His resurrection is actually our resurrection. To put it in a little more potentially offensive way—Because of your faith in Christ—We are as raised from the dead as is Jesus because it is actually His resurrection. It's not like He was raised and shared then some of that with us. That's not it. The Bible says we were raised together with Christ. His resurrection is my resurrection.* [56] [referring to Ephesians 1:20] [You can view Johnson's entire message on *****Video 27***** @2:32]

Johnson continues (@5:30):

*When Jesus was raised from the dead, He didn't just do it for you. He did it AS you.* [57]

And lastly (@36:28), we hear this from Bill Johnson:

*Until we all come to the unity of the faith and the knowledge of the son of God. Too many people think they know but they don't know. To the knowledge of the son of God to a perfect man. Millions and millions of body members come to a singular perfect man. . . until we share a knowledge, a full revelation of the person of Jesus—what He's like, how He is, to a perfect, mature man to the measure of the stature, equal measure to the stature of the fullness of Christ. To think that God would return for a weak and sick church and heal her when He gets her home is an offense to what He accomplished at the cross.*

*He made something possible that must be experienced. And before this thing is over, there will be a generation that says, "Yes, yes, yes, yes". . . so that a clear manifestation of this resurrected Christ is seen worldwide.* [58]

As you can see, the doctrines of Kenosis and the Manifestation of the Sons of God are intertwined. The goals are to achieve the status of "little gods." This is especially revealing due to what Mishel McCumber brings to light in her powerful book, *The View Beneath.*

> *All occult doctrine comes from the same source and is, in its most succinct form, the embodiment of what the serpent promised Eve in the Garden of Eden. He promised her that her eyes would be opened (attainment of gnosis), that she would not die (attainment of immortality), and that she would be like God (attainment of divinity).*[59] [All three are the ultimate goals of the New Apostolic Reformation.]

Likewise, the Sons of God doctrine lines up with the New Age beliefs according to Alice Bailey, New Age practitioner:

> *The Christ is being born today in many a human being, and increasingly will the sons of God appear in their true nature, to take over the guidance of humanity in the New Age.*[60]

Not all NAR leaders teach the entire Manifestation of the Sons of God doctrine. There are some variations among the churches. But those who do, don't announce fully their MSOG beliefs, or what is really behind their agenda. Surely they remember what happened in the 40's when followers were much more transparent about their unorthodox beliefs and the results that followed. Because of their transparency, the Latter Rain followers were exposed and then temporarily dismantled. Hopefully if the reader has been involved in the NAR or exposed to it, you can see in this section—the heretical overtones and false belief system seeping through the quotes and information, and how it is affecting the church today. We think you will agree that the belief system is not based on anything scriptural. In fact, it is at the core of occult doctrine.

On the contrary, we believe that Paul is very clear—that Christian believers cannot reach, evolve or achieve any change through special anointing, impartation, warfare, or any other way. We also believe that the Bible mentions nothing about an elite group, but that we all will receive our glorified bodies from Jesus Christ Himself only when He returns.

> ***Behold, I tell you a mystery; we will not all sleep, but we will all be changed, in a moment, in the twinkling***

*of an eye, at the last trumpet; for the trumpet will*
*sound, and the dead will be raised imperishable, AND*
*WE WILL BE CHANGED.* II Timothy 4:3-5

## Conclusion

To sum up this section on false doctrines, we include another quote by Alice Bailey who presents the New Age definition of the prime work of the church in her book, *The Externalization of the Hierarchy*:

> *The prime work of the church is to teach, and teach ceaselessly, preserving the outer appearance in order to reach the many who are accustomed to church usages. Teachers must be trained; Bible knowledge must be spread; the sacraments must be mystically interpreted, and the power of the church to heal must be demonstrated.*"[61]

Is Bill Johnson and other leaders of the New Apostolic Reformation willingly or unwillingly playing into the global agenda of the New Age movement thus fulfilling their vision and cause?

Unfortunately, Johnson has become so popular that many Christians who are exposed to his teachings will take whatever he says at face value and believe them just because Bill Johnson says them—no matter how outrageous or unbiblical! How many believers will be good Bereans (Acts 17:11) and take the time to compare the words of Bill Johnson or any teacher against the Word of God? We are advised to "examine all things carefully," "be on the alert," and to be "careful that we are not deceived." Especially in light of the drastic and critical changes in theology regarding the divinity and nature of Jesus Christ taught at Bethel Church (and so many churches today), we hope the reader will take heed to Paul's warnings and diligently study the Word of God for yourself and allow the Holy Spirit to lead you and teach you.

*Make me know your ways, O LORD;*
*Teach me Your paths,*
*Lead me in Your truth and teach me,*
*For You are the God of my salvation.*
*For You I wait all the day.* Psalm 25:4-5

51

## Endnotes – False Doctrines:

1. Bill Johnson, *When Heaven Invades Earth*, Destiny Image Publishers, Inc., (Shippensburg, PA, 2003), p. 29
2. Ibid., p. 79
3. Bill Johnson, *Face to Face with God*, Charisma House, (Lake Mary, FL, 2007) p. 109
4. https://www.gotquestions.org/kenosis.html
5. Bill Johnson, *The Supernatural Power of a Transformed Mind*, Destiny Image Publishers, Inc. (Shippensburg, PA, 2005), p. 50
6. Bob DeWaay, Echo Zoe Ministries blog of February 24, 2012 https://www.echzoe.com/archives/2509
7. Don Pirozok, *Kingdom Come*, Pilgrims Progress Publishing, (Spokane Valley, WA, 2016), p. 104
8. https:www.youtube.com/watch?v=DymOl71yMlw&feature=youtu.be **\*Video#1\***
9. Op cit., *When Heaven Invades Earth*, p. 57
10. Ibid., p. 57
11. https://www.lighthousetrailsresearch.com/blog/?p=3028760 quoting Alice Bailey, from their new booklet, *Dominionism, Kingdom Now & What Does the Bible Say?* written by Mike Oppenheimer
12. Op cit., *Kingdom Come*, p. 113
13. Dave Hunt & T. A. McMahon, *The Seduction of Christianity,* Harvest House Publishers, (Eugene, Oregon, 1985), p. 24-26
14. Ibid., p. 26
15. Ibid., p. 88
16. Ibid., p. 97
17. Judy Franklin & Ellyn Davis, *The Physics of Heaven*, Double Portion Publishing, (Crossville, TN, 2012), p. 128
18. Op cit., *When Heaven Invades Earth*, p. 138
19. Christian Research Network, April 16, 2018 quoting Rick Becker, Normalizing Mysticism http://christianresearchnetwork.org/2018/04/16/bethel-school-of-supernatural-ministry-normalizing-mysticism/
20. https://www.youtube.com/watch?v=EhG1x4fOtBw **\*Video#2\***
21. https://krisvallotton.com/8-signs-of-a-wealthy-mindset/ April 26, 2017
22. https://www.youtube.com/watch?v=7WboWrp-Cwo **\*Video 24\***
23. Ibid. **\*Video 24\***
24. Al Dager, *Vengence is Ours, The Church in Dominion,* Sword Publishers, (Redmond, WA, 1990), p. 44
25. Ibid., p. 87

26. C. Peter Wagner, *Dominion*, Chosen Books, (Grand Rapids, MI, 2008), p. 61
27. Ibid., p. 61
28. https://krisvallotton.com/my-8-eschatological-core-values/
29. Twitter posted by Kris Vallotton, October 15, 2016
    https://twitter.com/kvministries/status/787458684725190656  **\*Video#2\***
30. YouTube Video—The Last Days Ministries\*Laura\*, Heretic Bill Johnson Says Jesus Was Born Again  https://www.youtube.com/watch?v=BlpVvz63IAg **\*Video#3\***
31. Michael G. Moriarty, *The New Charismatics*, Zondervon Publishing House, (Grand Rapids, MI, 1992), p. 80 quoting [Daniel Ray McConnell, The Kenyon Connection: A Theological and Historical Analysis of the Cultic Origins of the Faith Movement,Thesis submitted to the theological
32. Op cit., Bob DeWaay, Echo Zoe Ministries blog of February 24, 2012
33. Op cit., *When Heaven Invades Earth*, p. 130
34. Op cit., *The Supernatural Power of a Transformed Mind*, 66
35. Op Cit., *When Heaven Invades Earth*, p. 76
36. Op cit., *The Supernatural Power of a Transformed Mind*, p. 68-69
37. Ibid., p. 73
38. Ibid., p. 65
39. Op cit., *When Heaven Invades Earth*, p. 129
40. Ibid., p. 84
41. Ibid., p. 87
42. Ibid., p. 93
43. Ibid., p. 94
44. Op cit., *The Supernatural Power of a Transformed Mind*, p. 75-76
45. Op cit., *When Heaven Invades Earth*, p. 84
45a. https://www.youtube.com/watch?v=vbEpJU1UMR0&feature=youtu.be **Video#11**
46. Rick Becker, On-line Article Famine in the Land Ministry, *Normalizing Mysticism*
47. Ibid.
48. Op cit.,*The New Charismatics*, 75-76
49. https://en.wikipedia.org/wiki/Latter_Rain_(post%E2%80%93World_War_II Movement)
50. Op cit., *When Heaven Invades Earth*, p. 149
51. Ibid., p. 184
52. Johnny Enlow, *The Seven Mountain Prophecy*: Unveiling the Coming Elijah Revolution, Creation House, (Lake Murray, FL, 2008), p. 24
53. Op cit., *The New Charismatics*, p. 74-75
54. Ibid., p. 75
55. https://churchwatchcentral.com/2017/05/28/bethel-church-peddling-new-breed-heresy-part-1-spirit-of-sonship-spirit-of-doption/?fbclid=IwAR2RRdXC7Q1s2_Lh29-kWxgcq9MrN9FDPCbLhEC8NJgc2FGRCFfBl-Afhqc56.
56.https://www.youtube.com/watch?v=jFpeVhqhnlw&fbclid=IwAR0ErXnKGIBRM3eLwE WF97Qm4npFm24-wpD0VZ2HhxplautchersXGMzxuc **\*Video#27\***
57. Ibid.
58. Ibid.
59. Mishel McCumber, *The View Beneath*, Mighty Roar Books, (Canada, 2016), p. 207
60. Op cit., Lighthouse Trails Publishing, Dominionism, Kingdom Now & What Does the Bible Say? written by Mike Oppenheimer          61. Ibid.

# V. New Age Fascination

*Many prominent pastors and conference speakers add fuel to the fire of fear by assuming that because the New Age promotes it, its origins must be from the devil. I find that form of reasoning weak at best. If we follow that line of thought, we will continue to give the devil the tools that God has given us for success in life and ministry.*[1]--Bill Johnson

In the above quote, is Bill Johnson suggesting that he thinks non-NAR pastors and church leaders are walking in fear if they reject New Age beliefs because the non-NAR leaders assume that the origins might be from the devil? There is nothing before or after this statement that explains his belief and, of course, he gives no example of how any New Age practices or beliefs can even remotely come from God, or how we can give the devil the tools that God has given us.

In addition, Johnson does not define or make clear just what tools he is talking about; but apparently, he believes that the tools have value. We will describe some of the "tools" that are being used at Bethel Church to experience spiritual encounters, receive counterfeit power through angels, receive new revelation or mantles from the dead, connect to the sound of heaven, take trips to heaven and more—all of which are associated with Gnosticism and the New Age rather than biblical Christianity.

Because the dangers of the New Age are not often taught in Christian churches anymore, we are often asked, "What is the New Age Movement about?" One definition can be found in the book, *For Many Shall Come in My Name* by Ray Yungen:

> *Individuals who, in the context of historical occultism are in mystical contact with unseen sources and dimensions; who receive guidance and direction from these dimensions, and most importantly, who promote this state-of-being to the rest of humanity.*[2]

New Agers believe that everything is made up of energy, even God. To New Agers, everything is God—even human beings. There is no distinction between God being outside of us, or that He is only a "presence" that lives within. The goal of the New Age is that one can achieve access to this "presence" within, connect to the higher self, and become one with the universe. New Agers believe that, in order to do this, one needs to awaken the higher self so that transformation can occur.

Another goal of the New Age is to advance through different levels to experience the God within so much so that one can receive ancient hidden secrets and knowledge daily from their "masters" and other unknown sources. The absolute goal is to achieve Christ consciousness. Lastly, the agenda of the New Age is to infiltrate churches and all society. They want to bring peace and enlightenment to the world through one's acceptance and practice of their beliefs.

The New Age Movement has many similarities to the New Apostolic Movement. They both have tens of thousands of networks and organizations all working for world unity based upon religious experiences and beliefs that have their roots in the occult and Eastern mysticism. They both are on a mission and believe that they have a mandate to teach that the "old" has become stale and unexciting while suggesting that God has "new" revelation for us today. Constance Cumby in her timeless book, *The Hidden Dangers of the Rainbow*, tells us more:

> *Their primary goal or the secret behind their unity-in-diversity is the formation of a New World Order. The Movement usually operates on the basis of a well-formulated body of underlying esoteric or occult teachings. . . It has successfully infiltrated nearly every segment of our personal, religious, and professional lives. The glue binding most New Age devotees is one of common mystical experiences. "Experiential religion" is considered vital within the Movement.[3]*

An article from Inspiredwalk.com tells us the true agenda of the New Age Movement:

> *One of the main agendas of the New Age Movement is to become the dominant religion or lifestyle within the entire world. Therefore, in order for New Age philosophies to become dominant, then all other religions especially Christianity must either be destroyed or become less of a spiritual influence within society and in the individual lives of people.[4]*

Other similarities with the NAR and the New Age is their glorification and dependence on occult practices such as: communication with the dead, astral projection (leaving one's body in the spirit realm and traveling to some other place on earth), conversations and fascination with angels and demons, receiving hidden, secret knowledge other than from our five senses, to name a few. Both movements aspire to the elimination of Christianity (that has been passed down for two thousand years) as we know it today. They both also believe that the church needs to be reformed.

Bear these things in mind as you continue to read this book. You will see how easy it is to understand where some of these "new" ideas that have crept into the church have come from and why we, and so many discerning Christians, are warning the body of Christ to beware and to be aware.

## "Physics of Heaven – *Exploring God's Mysteries of Sound, Light, Energy, Vibrations, and Quantum Physics.*"

Not too long ago, it was a common practice in the church to warn its members about the dangers of New Age. Today not only are Christians not being warned, but a segment of the church is actually actively engaging in its beliefs and practices. Nothing is as apparent as the very dangerous and disturbing book, *The Physics of Heaven*. The book shows what Bethel Church aspires to and where they are leading the body of Christ.

In 2011, Judy Franklin, along with Ellyn Davis wrote the book, *The Physics of Heaven*. Judy Franklin is the administrative assistant to Bill Johnson. Ellyn Davis describes her desire "to bridge the gap between Christianity and the discoveries of quantum physics as well as discover God's truths hidden in quantum mysticism and the New Age." That's enough to make you pause right there. But the book also contains chapters written by other authors including Bill Johnson who wrote two chapters in the book, and Bill Johnson's wife, Beni, who wrote one of them. Some of the chapter titles in *The Physics of Heaven* include subjects such as:

*Vibrating in Harmony with God*
*Sound of Heaven*
*Quantum Mysticism*
*Human Body Frequencies*

One wonders why a Christian would need to learn about such topics as: sound, vibrations, mysticism or frequencies, or even have the remotest curiosity about them. In the *Foreword* to the book, Kris Vallotton, Senior Associate Leader at Bethel writes this:

> *If you are tired of being a settler, existing on the shores of tradition and riskless living, this book is for you. But beware, because once you get a taste of these authors' insights into light, sound, vibration and quantum physics and you discover how God has written His personal story into creation, you are destined to see the Almighty all around you. Like listening to surround sound while watching a great movie, this book will awaken nature's voice in you, curing deafness that was predicated long ago by single dimensional thinking.*[5]

Vallotton makes no explanation or gives no scriptural reference as to what he is referring to by "single dimensional thinking." In fact, the book is not a reflection of anything even close to New Testament Christianity. Almost every page in every chapter embraces New Age and Hindu beliefs and practices. One such chapter is on the "Zero-Point Field." Judy Franklin likens the power of Almighty God to a "sea of quantum light":

> *I began to understand that if this world is actually going to be what it was created to be in the beginning, now that Jesus has redeemed everything, we need to know what this power is, this "sea of quantum light" that undergirds everything. And, more importantly, we need to know how to access it.*[6]

The Bible tells us everything we need to know about light and also how to access the Light of life—the Lord Jesus Christ:

*I am the Light of the world; he who follows Me will not walk in the darkness, but will have the Light of life.* John 8:12

*Your eye is the lamp of your body. When your vision is clear, your whole body also is full of light. But when it is poor, your body is full of darkness. See to it then that the light within you is not darkness.* Luke 11:34-35.

*Woe to those who call evil good and good evil; who turn darkness to light and light to darkness; who replace bitter with sweet and sweet with bitter.* Isaiah 5:20.

At the beginning of the book, there is a kind of disclaimer entitled, "A Habitation of Dragons" (interesting choice of words) written by Franklin and Davis. They compare the topics in their book to the unexplored happenings of Christians gone before them, and also the uncharted, unknown territories that the ancient explorers (such as Cortez and Magellan) were willing to go to in the past. The pursuits of the early Christians and explorers eventually led them to find new lands and riches that they led future generations to. The implication is that we shouldn't be afraid of unknown or unfamiliar dragons but, at the same time, they admit that some of the information in their book might be "scary to explore."

Also Franklin expresses in the "Introduction" that she believes that "what the Lord has been showing both of us is the **absolute truth that will help us bring God's kingdom to this earth.** The Lord is ready to use sound, light, and energy in ways we never dreamed, but we first need to have some foundational understandings." [emphasis ours]. Is she suggesting that believers in the Lord Jesus Christ need the "absolute truths" in her book because the authors are going to show information that we've never seen before?

In another chapter, Ellyn Davis talks about her move to Sedona, Arizona, and tells us that what she heard and saw there from the New Agers' teaching can be backed up with the Scriptures:

58

*I was intrigued by what I found there. I saw healings and mystical experiences and revelations to rival anything I had seen or experienced in the church. . . It wasn't that I wanted to become a New Ager, I just wanted to find out if maybe they had uncovered some truths the church hadn't. The strange thing was, much of what I saw and heard embodied biblical principles and could be backed up by Scripture.* [7]

Davis makes a claim but gives no specific examples of how anything in the New Age can be backed up by the Scriptures to substantiate her statement. To the contrary, in II Corinthians 6:14-18, Paul says this:

> **Do not be bound together with unbelievers; for what partnership have righteousness and lawlessness, or what fellowship has light with darkness? . . .**
>
> **Therefore, COME OUT FROM THEIR MIDST AND BE SEPARATE," says the Lord.**
> **AND DO NOT TOUCH WHAT IS UNCLEAN;**
> **And I will welcome you.**
> **And I will be a father to you,**
> **And you shall be sons and daughters to Me,"**
> **Says the Lord Almighty.**

Note: In the verse, *AND DO NOT TOUCH WHAT IS UNCLEAN* above, the Greek word *unclean* is *akathartos* (Strong's #169). It means *impure because wrongly mixed* (biblehub.com). Glorification of New Age is just that—attempting to wrongly mix Christianity with the occult.

> **This is the message we have heard from Him and announce to you, that God is Light and in Him there is no darkness at all.** I John 1:5

Ellyn Davis goes on to share about the need for Christians to take back truths from the New Age that belong to Christians. **Ellyn also admits that the revelations that they are receiving and teaching line up with the New Age:**

*At that time, I could not find a single Christian leader who shared a similar interest in finding out if there were truths hidden in the New Age. Now we are beginning to hear more and more revelation that is in line with what New Agers have been saying all along and we are hearing more and more teaching about Christians "taking back truths" from the New Age that really belong to citizens of the Kingdom of God.*[8]

**For He rescued us from the domain of darkness, and transferred us to the kingdom of His beloved Son.** Colossians 1:13

Furthermore, she goes on to express that she and all of the other writers of the book believe that there are **"precious"** truths hidden in the New Age that belong to Christians, and the traditional, biblical values of the past are like "dove dung.":

*I believe that the Holy Spirit is moving again. So do all of the Christian leaders who contributed to this book. They are all trying to position themselves to be "where the puck is going to be," not where it's been.*

*None of them want to be caught in the "dove dung" left behind when the Spirit moves on. They all agree that the next move of God will cause a shift at the deepest level of who we are—perhaps at the very "vibrational level" that the New Age movement has been exploring. They also all agree that there are precious truths hidden in the New Age that belong to us as Christians and need to be extracted from the worthless.*[9] [emphasis ours].

Please understand what Ellyn Davis is saying. She is admitting that all the contributing authors, which include Bill Johnson, agree that there are precious truths hidden in the New Age that Christians need. This leaves no doubt as to what the leaders of Bethel Church believe. It is difficult to understand how any Bible believing Christian can defend Johnson and continue to follow his teachings, even when presented with this fact. Yet, unfortunately, many do.

60

Apparently, the Bible is not enough. The authors of The *Physics of Heaven* continuously express in their book that we need to go searching in the New Age for mysteries and new revelation knowledge because this knowledge has been hidden and lost throughout the centuries. The need for this so-called knowledge is nothing but Gnosticism revisited—a belief system that has been around since the early church. Gnosticism is totally opposite to what the Scriptures teach us. The Light shines into the darkness, the darkness does NOT shine into the Light.

> *In the beginning was the Word, and the Word was with God, and the Word was God. He was in the beginning with God. All things came into being through Him, and apart from Him nothing came into being that has come into being. In Him was life, and the life was the Light of men. The Light shines in the darkness, and the darkness did not comprehend it.* John 1:1-5

Another topic expressed continuously in the book is the importance of sound. Bill Johnson's wife, Beni, tells us this about the "sound of heaven":

> *When you connect to the spirit realm, you make an alliance with that sound of heaven and all things move to that sound. I love the feeling that I get when I know that I have connected with God and can release heaven's sound over situations. That is when I know change is at hand.*[10]

> *Take time to be alone and listen and wait for His sound to come to your spirit. As you deliberately shift your attention, you can physically feel Him stirring in your innermost being, changing and shifting you. The vibrations of heaven are a powerful life-changing substance. Anything is possible when you plug in.*[11]

Even though this is just a brief overview, we have shown that the book, *The Physics of Heaven*, by their own admission, aligns more with New Age beliefs (that are opposed to biblical Christianity) than the Word of God. As Christians, we emphatically understand that there is nothing in the New Age belief system or practices that we want or need.

The bottom line is: Do we believe the Scriptures are true? Do we believe in the finished work of Jesus Christ on the cross? Do we believe that the Bible is complete? Or do we believe that we need to go to the dark side so that we can find "hidden mysteries" and "new revelation" from the New Age that was stolen from the church—and receive a mixture? We can find the answers in the following Scriptures—

> *The things you have learned and received and heard and seen in me, practice these things, and the God of peace will be with you.* Philippians 4:9

> *See to it that no one takes you captive through philosophy and empty deception, according to the tradition of men, according to the elementary principles of the world, rather than according to Christ. For in Him all the fullness of Deity dwells in bodily form, and in Him you have been made complete, and He is the head over all rule and authority.* Colossians 2:8-10

> *Beloved, while I was making every effort to write you about our common salvation, I felt the necessity to write to you appealing that you contend earnestly for the faith which was once for all handed down to the saints.* Jude 9

## Shawn Bolz & "Prophetic" words received from the dead

Shawn Bolz, a highly respected "prophet" throughout the New Apostolic Reformation, is a frequent guest at Bethel Church and the Bethel School of Supernatural Ministry. When prophesying, he often calls out something specific about a person such as their name or address in order to identify who it is that he perceives he is receiving "words of knowledge" for. After the person is identified in the meeting, he proceeds to give that person "prophetic words" that he believes he is receiving from God.

When Bolz was speaking at a leaders' conference at Bethel Church, Bill Johnson and the large congregation of people witnessed him supposedly communicating with recently **deceased** NAR "Prophet" Bob Jones and Bill Johnson's **deceased** father. He shared that he was receiving messages from "heaven" about Bill Johnson and reported to Bill and the congregation about what he perceived to be seeing and hearing. He excused what was happening as not being *necromancy* ("a method of divination through invocation of the dead.") [Definition taken from Webster's Universal College Dictionary].

He also admits that his encounter and prophetic words are "outside the box," yet simply defends the practice because he claims that he was not pursuing it, and that he was "just seeing a vision of what is already happening around Jesus." He defended his visionary experience by saying that he is a Christian, and that he "only believes in the Word of God. " Then why is he receiving messages from the dead?

He never talked about "testing the spirits" as we are biblically instructed to do, or attempted to discern as to whether or not his encounter was, indeed, from God. Does Bolz believe that just because he is a Christian that he is prevented from hearing anything else but the voice of God? He can try to defend the practice any way he wants, and profess to believe in the Word of God. But the Bible is clear. We are not to communicate with the dead because it is detestable to the Lord. Period.

> *There shall not be found among you anyone who makes his son or his daughter pass through the fire, one who uses divination, one who practices witchcraft, or one who interprets omens, or a sorcerer, or one who casts a spell, or a medium, or a spiritist, or one who calls up the dead. For whoever does these things is detestable to the Lord. Deut. 18:10-12*
>
> *When they say to you, "Consult the mediums and the spiritists, who whisper and mutter," should not a people consult their God? Should they consult the*

*dead on behalf of the living? To the law and to the testimony! If they do not speak according to this word, it is because they have no dawn.* Isaiah 8:19 (Also please refer to Jeremiah 14:14 and Ezekiel 13:9.)

Bolz went on to tell Bill Johnson that Bob Jones and Bill's dad were "interceding in heaven to bring the next purpose." Bolz then told Bill that they (Bob Jones and Bill's father) were "so excited and talking like 100 miles an hour." Bolz continued to report that Bill's grandfather was there also, "leading a heavenly choir in heaven" as were several of Johnson's ancestors. Bolz was also receiving messages from deceased "Prophet" Bob Jones who told Bolz the following about Bill Johnson:

> *And I saw heaven crying out for the deposits to be released. Money has been reserved that is accessible now and it's going to blow you away.* [12] **\*Video #4\***

This entire scenario can be seen on the YouTube video: https://www.facebook.com/groups/276907005676141/search/?query= shawn%20bolz%20at%20bethel

In the book, *The Second Coming of the New Age* by Steven Bancarz and Josh Peck, we learn the definitions of channeling and mediumship:

> <u>Channeling</u> *is the practice whereby a human taps into an interdimensional being of some kind (believed to be a deceased person, alien, spirit guide, etc.) usually by entering a trance-like state of consciousness before attempting to make contact by reaching out to the being. Once the person makes contact, then he or she acts as a conduit for the being to convey specific messages to the human race. In other words, the person becomes a "vessel" through which a foreign consciousness can speak.*

> <u>Mediumship</u> *is a similar practice wherein rather than acting as a "channel" for another entity to speak through, the "medium" initiates direct contact with those in the spirit world in the hopes of receiving wisdom and insight (usually about future events.)* [13]

Bancarz and Peck go on to tell us the truth about these practices which many discerning Christians believe is happening with most of the prophetic in the New Apostolic Reformation churches today.

*Since the Bible tells us that Satan masquerades as an angel of light (2 Corinthians 11:14), it can be argued that the spiritual powers behind the mediums and the channelers are demonic entities impersonating deceased persons, spirits, and other beings— demons putting on a show to lead people into spiritual darkness and confusion, away from the true God....*[14]

Unfortunately, the "apostles" and "prophets" in the hyper-charismatic churches have turned the gift of prophecy into fortune-telling and clairvoyance. Michael Moriarty, in his book, *The New Charismatics,* writes this about channeling prophetic messages:

*Upon close inspection, many discernible patterns emerge when comparing the techniques used by many of the new charismatics, particularly those who operate as prophets, with those employed by New Age channelers. The same technique is used and taught by many charismatic prophets. Although their aim is to channel a message from God, the meditative techniques used to bring this about bear little resemblance to the biblical prophets, but remarkable similarity to those used by a New Age guru.*[15]

Also the prophets are taught that the words that they speak have to be positive. In fact, much of what they "prophesy" is about "self" because what they speak, to whom they are prophesying, is often about: one's destiny, one's spiritual gifts, and how wonderful the person is. Their words are rarely about repentance and forgiveness of sin.

We close with the following very concerning statement by Shawn Bolz that was posted on his Facebook page accessed on 6/23/19.

*Because prophesy, at times, has been a controversial subject, I want to ask you a favor: suspend your caution and concern, and open your heart and mind to some new ideas—especially some new experiences.*

You can see by this statement that he, too, is subtly brainwashing his followers by telling them to turn off their discernment, and receive "new" ideas and experiences. This is clearly in opposition to what we are instructed to do throughout the New Testament. We are never told to suspend caution but, on the contrary, are emphatically told to "test the spirits," "be sober," "be on the alert," and "to guard the treasure that has been entrusted to us." This is yet another example of how unsuspecting, undiscerning Christians are being led away from the Bible into an experiential and mystical version of Christianity.

## Christ Alignment, Destiny Readings and "Spirit" Pants

In December of 2017, a couple named Ken and Jen Hodge from Melbourne, Australia and their ministry, Christ Alignment, was exposed. It was reported that Christ Alignment is a ministry that visits New Age and "queer" festivals doing "spiritual readings" using what they call "destiny cards." Although denied by the Hodges, the cards look much like tarot cards and are used in the same way.

The Hodges claim that they are a deliverance ministry aimed at rescuing New Agers out of darkness and leading people into Christ's salvation. Yet when the many people that we viewed who were interviewed on their internet website, www.christalignment.org/ talked about their experiences with spiritual readings, nothing was mentioned about Jesus Christ and Him crucified, nor did they give any glory to Jesus for their salvation. The testimonies did suggest that the people who participated in the "readings" believed that they had a genuine spiritual experience, however.

The Hodges advertise on their website that:

> The Christ Alignment can choose from at least seven different types of cards which have been made by us for our destiny readings. These are not necessary for an effective reader, as we are all hearing from the 2rd heaven realm, but greatly enhance the reading.

> We believe they are more productive and higher than other card readings as they are our own and can address every current life question that you may have. Card readings with Christ Alignment are always followed by the reader taking the client into a deep encounter using a much higher realm. Often color is seen and it's in this realm that answers come for poignant life's questions that clients have and lives are changed.

Theresa Dedmon, who is on the pastoral staff at Bethel (where she oversees the Creative Arts Department for the church and Bethel School of Supernatural Ministry) designs and uses destiny cards. Unlike the Hodges, she says she does not use destiny cards to tell people's future or give people readings. She says that she uses them instead "to encourage people, give them hope and lead them to Christ." Dedmon wrote the book, *Born to Create, Stepping into Supernatural Destiny* in which Bill Johnson wrote the Foreword, and Kris Vallotton, along with other Bethel staff members have endorsed the book. She says this in Chapter 7, *Releasing Supernatural Creativity in the Church:*

> *Supernatural Creativity can impact people who are coming to your church for the first time. During the school year, I have the School of Ministry students sit at Bethel's welcome table and prophesy to newcomers through **destiny cards**, singing and playing instruments over people.*[16]

On-line ministry, *The Azuza Report* of December 20, 2017, says this about prophesying through destiny cards:

> *God speaks through people not cards. No "cheat sheet" for the prophetic. This leads to all types of false prophesies, divination and, in some cases, complete sorcery. Prophecy is from God and is spoken in the right moment to the right person about the right issue. This idea of cookie cutter words from the Lord that we see coming out of some ministries is not the prophetic word of the Lord. It is just what the Bible calls "vain imagination."*[17]

*Azuza Report* continues:

> *The truth is that we are being more impacted by the world than the world is being impacted by us. Redeeming worldly concepts to make them sacred is not the great commission. We are to change the world, not throw a little Jesus on their culture and call it "redeemed.*[18]

In addition, Theresa Dedmon has a line of fashion for sale that she designs. She says that if you wear her pants, it "will enhance your awareness of God's presence" and more.

*My fashion designs embody the prophetic art they are created from. Wearing my art enhances your awareness of God's presence, and helps you become a walking encounter of Heaven's message to those around you.* [19]

## Trips to Heaven

Taking trips to heaven is a practice that is taught and encouraged by many leaders and teachers in the New Apostolic Reformation including Bethel Church. In doing so, some visit heaven through visions, or trances. But others say they actually leave their bodies in order to travel to heaven to receive messages from departed saints and/or loved ones. In the occult world, this practice is known as spirit travel or astral projection.

Even the children at Bethel are trained to "go to heaven" and are reported to "hang out there." They are being taught to pray for arms to grow out, and they practice raising people from the dead. Bethel's Children's Leader, Deborah Reed confirms this practice:

> *Yes, we take our kids to heaven, who doesn't? People who know how to do heaven things take our kids to heaven. We also have "tour guides" who take our Middle Schoolers to heaven.* [20] ***Video #18*** (@8:20)

Some followers of the NAR take these trips on a daily basis. In fact, instructional courses are taught as to how to do it. Acts 8:39 is given as the Bible verse to justify the practice of trips to heaven by people of the NAR where the Bible describes Philip as being "snatched away." But this experience is only mentioned once in the Book of Acts, and it was totally a God thing in that Philip did not seek out the experience. He did not spend time "soaking," nor did he take a course about how to do it. It was totally a spontaneous act by the Holy Spirit for a specific purpose.

The following video speaks for itself. NAR "Prophet" Bob Jones, was a regular speaker at Bethel Church before he passed away. You can actually watch him lead an entire Bethel Church congregation on how to take such a trip to heaven in this very disturbing video: YouTube: https://www.youtube.com/watch?v=TYgOn_MWpzo ***Video #5***

Some more examples are found on a blog dated 10/7/13 entitled *Kris Vallotton — 4 Voices and Languages of God: Visions and Dreams* which was found on the Bethel School of Supernatural Ministry blogspot. It was reported that Kris Vallotton has led those in his services to go into trances for the purpose of connecting with the dead.

*1) Kris is invited to a town devastated by a string of 5 deaths among teenagers who committed suicide in Oregon. He was asked to speak about life. A lady who sat alone in despair in the distance all three days. She joined them for the last session when Kris spoke on "Go can do anything." She challenged Chris and explained her son was one of the five that was dead. He heard the Holy Spirit say, "ask her if she wants to meet her son." He asked her and she said yes but not understanding what that meant. She fell back hard on the ground and entered a 3 hour vision. When she came out she joyfully shared how God took her to heaven and was comforted by her son that he was fine.* [text left unedited]

*2) Kris was praying for people and saw a lady and knew she had 7 abortions. He spoke life over her and as he prophesied over her she explained she had 7 abortions. He asked if he would like to meet these babies. She soon went into a trance and had a vision of heaven where she met these 7 little ones who had died. Kris explained this has happened many other times.*[21]

There is so much that can be said about these two scenarios. First of all, Vallotton assumed that the voice he heard was the Holy Spirit. Why would the Holy Spirit ask him to do/say something that is blatantly against the Word of God where it is strictly forbidden to communicate with the dead—and is detestable to Him? (Deuteronomy 17:9)

Does Vallotton believes that it's alright to go into trances like the above experiences because Peter went in a trance (Acts 10:9-11), Paul experienced a trance (Acts 22:17-21), and also John (Revelation 1:10)? But the purpose of these trances in the New Testament were not to speak to dead people. Again, in all three of these situations, God wanted to give to these men of God strategic and specific instructions.

God does not want to or need to speak to us through dead people. He is the God of the living. We hear a lot about faith from the people of the NAR. But where is their faith when it comes to praying and believing that

He will give to us generously all that we need without looking outside of Him through trips to heaven, connecting to the dead and other such practices?

## Alabaster House Prayer Center

The prayer center at Bethel Church is called the Alabaster House Prayer Center. What's unique about this prayer center is that it has a pyramid on the top of the building that glows red at night. It is difficult to understand why a Christian ministry would choose to put a pyramid (a well-known occult symbol) on top of a building used for prayer. However, the description on their website gives us some explanation:

> *The Alabaster Prayer House and surrounding gardens is a quiet and peaceful place to be in contemplative prayer and enjoy God's presence. It is open 24 hours a day every day for people to encounter the presence of God. All are welcome.* [22]

Most unaware Christians would not discern anything wrong with the above description of a ministry prayer center. But what is **contemplative prayer** described here? On Bethel website, they explain about the value of *soaking* (another term used for contemplative prayer):

> *Encountering the intimate presence of God is the gateway to the supernatural! When we soak in His presence, we are radically transformed into His likeness. We learn to hear His voice, we learn to see Him, and we are anointed to walk in miracles, signs, and wonders.*
>
> *For some, soaking opens up the door to visions, angelic visitations, or out-of-body experiences. Others have physical manifestations of electricity, heat, weeping, and more. Whether or not we dramatically experience the spirit realm or physical manifestations, we get to receive the greatest gift: His presence. When we stop and spend time with Him, we receive a deposit of His Spirit in our innermost being, renewing and strengthening us to fulfill our destinies.* [23]

As opposed to fundamental Christianity where one seeks Almighty God, the Creator of all things who is outside of one's self—in contemplative prayer, one seeks a God who is inside by emptying the mind of its own thoughts and looking deeply to find the God within (whoever or whatever that may be). Contemplative prayer is also called listening prayer, breath prayer, or centering prayer. Its roots come from the Desert Fathers who were Catholic monks who lived a life of solitude, and did not want to be distracted by the world. Most New Agers, and people in the occult practice this type of praying. The website, *GotQuestions.org* defines contemplative prayer like this:

> *The purpose is to clear one's mind of outside concerns so that God's voice may be more easily heard. After the centering prayer, the practitioner is to sit still, listen for direct guidance from God, and feel His presence.* [24]

Professor Johan Malan, University of Limpopo, South Africa describes the dangers of contemplative prayer and offers the following information:

> *Contemplating God's Word is a good thing. But the contemplative prayer I speak of is not. First practised by Monks centuries ago, it died out and did not re-enter again until the 1960s when Catholic monks, Thomas Keating and Thomas Merton, decided to introduce the practice to mainstream Christianity.*

> *Richard Foster, a supporter of contemplative prayer, writes a curious warning about this practice in his book, Prayer: Finding the Heart's True Home: 'I also want to give a word of precaution. In the silent contemplation of God we are entering deeply into the spiritual realm, and there is such a thing as a supernatural guidance... While the Bible does not give us a lot of information on that, there are various orders of spiritual beings, and some of them are definitely not in cooperation with God and his way! ... But for now I want to encourage you to learn and practice prayers of protection.'*

> *Then why do it, Mr. Foster? Why would God put me in a position to fend for myself in this unknown spiritual realm surrounded by spiritual beings that are not in cooperation with God and his way? He would not.* [25]

For participants of contemplative prayer, the focus of experiencing God becomes the preferred and relevant way to hear from Him. God certainly

71

speaks to his children, but Jesus did not model anything that even remotely resembles the practice of contemplative prayer.

> *Do not be anxious about anything, but in everything, by prayer and petition, with thanksgiving, present your requests to God.* Philippians 4:6

Also we are not told anywhere in the Bible to clear our mind before we pray. To the contrary, Paul tells us this:

> *I will pray with my spirit, but I will also pray with my mind; I will sing with my spirit, but I will also sing with my mind.* I Corinthians 14:14

The further explanation of contemplative prayer from *GotQuestions.org* continues:

> . . . *Contemplative prayer, by design, focuses on having a mystical experience with God. Mysticism, however, is purely subjective, and does not rely upon truth or fact. . . What we know about God is based on fact; trusting in experiential knowledge over the biblical record takes a person outside of the standard that is the Bible.*
>
> *Contemplative prayer is no different than the meditative exercises used in Eastern religions and New Age cults. . . Contemplative prayer, as practiced in the modern prayer movement is in opposition to biblical Christianity and should definitely be avoided.*[26]

Christians who practice contemplative prayer justify the centering methods they use, because they say they are focusing on the Holy Spirit not the inner self like the New Agers do. But the fact that God lives inside of us doesn't mean that we need special access to His presence by special techniques. Contemplative prayer changes the traditional, biblical meaning of prayer: petitioning the Lord, praising Him, talking to Him, bringing a problem before Him, or asking for wisdom. Jesus talked to God the Father, made requests, and thanked Him. When the disciples asked Jesus how to pray, He gave them (and us) a clear model. He never asks us to sit still and to feel His presence.

Well meaning, but deceived Christians think that they are really participating in something spiritual when engaging in contemplative prayer. They believe that it is God talking to them and contemplative prayer is a means by which they can hear Him. On the contrary, many discerning Christians believe that contemplative prayer opens the door for practitioners to be in contact with and/or channel a counterfeit spirit other than the Holy Spirit. In fact, much of the heretical doctrines and false prophesies that are received in the hyper-charismatic church/New Apostolic Reformation are received during times of contemplative prayer. Some of the words that are expressed through the practitioners of this type of prayer are extra-biblical and contrary to the Scriptures.

Another reason contemplative prayer is dangerous is the fact that practitioners often experience a peaceful, euphoric feeling which causes him/her to keep going back for more. It is easy for one to become addicted to the experience so much so that it becomes more exciting and fulfilling than praying in a biblical way or reading the Bible.

In summary, Author Ray Yungen, explains contemplative prayer this way:

> *The answer to the contemplative prayer movement is simple. A Christian is complete in Christ. The argument that contemplative prayer can bring a fuller measure of God's love, guidance, direction, and nurturing is the epitome of dishonor to Jesus Christ, the Good Shepherd. It is, in essence, anti-Christian.*[27]

The subject of the Alabaster House Prayer Center would not be complete without the following outrageous statements taken from Beni Johnson's website where she talks about the prayer center. She says that "heavenly activity is present there" because she reports that people hear voices and laughter underneath the floor.

> *Just recently I was in my office, which is in the same building as the prayer house. My door was open, and a lady came out of the prayer room. She asked me if there was a room below the prayer room. I told her "No," and asked why? She told me that she kept hearing people laughing and talking. I told her that was normal, and that other people have heard that same thing. Being a visitor to Bethel, she was blown away, and it messed her up—in a good way. She was hearing the sound of heaven. We do hear the sound of heaven all around our prayer house. It always seems to be one*

*of joy and laughter. There seems to be a party going on. In my opinion, I think that heaven really likes to hang out in our prayer house.*[28]

## Beni Johnson and Waking Up Angels

No believer doubts the existence and importance of angels as God's holy messengers. The Bible shows us how, all throughout time, God used them to communicate his plans for His children. But encounters with angels were very few and far between in both Testaments of the Bible in a believer's every-day life. Yet today, at Bethel Church and in the New Apostolic Reformation, many are fascinated and heavily focused on angels. They profess to speak to them daily, receive information from them, are dependent on them for healing and certain power; and they believe that they, as believers, have the authority to "release" angels to perform different ministry functions. In comparison, angels are very popular in the New Age, as well. John Ankerberg and John Weldon in their *Encylopedia of New Age Beliefs* tell us the following about angels and the New Age:

> *Angel contact, angel consciousness, and angel work refer to New Age forms of communication with alleged heavenly angels for purposes of spiritual assistance, developing altered states of consciousness, psychic powers, or fostering New Age goals, in general.*
>
> *New Age contact began as a logical extension of the modern channeling movement. Contact with alleged heavenly angels is said to be a part of an emerging planetary transformation of spirituality that will reveal man's true divine nature and unite him with the cosmos.*
>
> *Good angels are not being contacted in the popular angel revival; instead, demons or fallen angels, who masquerade as godly angels, are deceiving people by confusing the nature of the contacts.*[29]

Beni Johnson is director of Bethel's Prayer Center, ministry teams and the intercessors. She tells two stories on her blog post of 3/16/09 about

74

experiencing angels and the ability we have as Christians to "wake them up." A portion of the blog is reported here:

> One of our students came to our Supernatural School of Ministry from Wales. Before she moved here, she had a major encounter with God. She was woken in the middle of the night because the presence of God was so strong in her room. She could see a visible cloud in her room, and she waited on God to see what He was saying. Then God said to her, "I want you to go to Moriah Chapel and say, 'Wakey, Wakey.' She thought, "You want me to do what? I'm sorry God, but I'm not doing that!" Then He said to her again, "I want you to go to Moriah Chapel and say, 'Wakey, Wakey.' At that point, she knew that if she didn't do it, she would regret it for the rest of her life. The next day when she got to the chapel, there were a lot of people outside. She said normally the chapel was empty. She asked God why there were so many people there and He said to her, "Because I had to tell you twice." She stood outside of the chapel and whispered, "Wakey, Wakey" because she did not want anyone to hear her. God then said to her, "Is that how much you want revival in Wales?" She then stood there that day and yelled at the top of her lungs, "WAKEY, WAKEY"!!!

> Nothing happened for about five minutes, so she turned around to cross the road to go over to a shop. As she turned around, she felt the ground begin to shake and heard this huge yawn. She looked back at the chapel and a huge angel stepped out. All she could see were his feet because he was that large. She asked him who he was, and he turned to her and said, "I am the angel from the 1904 revival and you just woke me up." She asked him, "Why have you been asleep?" The angel answered and said, "Because no one has been calling out for revival anymore." She then asked him if he was the angel that was going to bring the next revival. He told her "No, because the next revival would bring in many more souls for the kingdom." Since the angel has awoken, he has been seen by many others around Wales. I don't know about you, but that would really get me excited! Having a visitation like that would really shake you up. I like angels. When you talk about them, they like to show up! And when they come, they bring the presence of God.[30]
*Video #6*

Nowhere in the Bible do we find angels that teach or explain doctrine. And nowhere does the Bible suggest that angels bring moves of God, or that we have the power to "release them" or to "wake them up." Beni continues on the same blog spot with another story about waking up angels—a personal "encounter." Although it reads like satire, it appears that she really believes that what she is receiving and experiencing is—from God.

*In the last couple of months, I personally have become more aware of the angelic activity in this realm. One of those times was when we were on a prayer trip to Arizona. A group of us had decided that it was time for us to take a prayer trip down to Sedona to release more of God's kingdom. In doing so, we rented an RV and drove from Redding, California, (where we live) all the way down to Sedona, Arizona. Along the way, we would stop and pray if we felt impressed to do so.*

*One morning as we were driving up over Tehachapi Pass and coming down into the Mojave Desert, I began to feel angels. The closer we got, the stronger the impression felt. I could see them everywhere! Whenever there are angels present, I get very animated and excited, knowing that God is up to something big. I announced this to the group and said, "We have got to stop! We have to stop somewhere." We found an exit, took it and drove into this little town. We didn't really know what to do or where to go. We just knew that something was going on and we needed to find out what. As we drove around a corner I said, "I think that we are going to wake up some angels here." No sooner had I said that— we drove past a hotel to our left; and, no joke, the name of the store was Moriah Country Inn.*

*When I saw that sign, we immediately remembered the 'Wakey, Wakey' story from Wales. We knew we were to turn around, get out of the RV and wake up the angels. I wish I could convey to you \*the energy and the quickness of how God was working. We jumped out of the RV, I blew the shofar and rang the bell, and we yelled, "WAKEY, WAKEY." We got back into the RV and drove off. As we drove off, hilarious laughter broke out! We were stunned at the speed at which this all took place, and were* *spinning from the adventure and the angelic activity. What in the world had just happened?! Heaven collided with earth. Woo hoo!!*

*Since that time, there has been a stirring in me to awaken the angels for use in this kingdom reign that is upon us here on earth. I have shared these two stories in other places and have done a prophetic act of waking up the angels having everybody cry out, "WAKEY, WAKEY!" I know it is strange, but it is very effective.*[31]
*Video #7*

## Beni Johnson and tuning forks of love

Beni Johnson believes that we can use tuning forks for the purpose of healing. Scripture, please!

*I was talking with Ray Hughes the other day and was telling him about using a 528 HZ tuning fork as a prophetic act. Someone told me that this tuning fork is called the tuning fork of LOVE. Google it. Ray told me that science has said that this fork is the sound that holds earth. That blew me away"!! One thing about this 528 Hz tuning fork is that science tells us that the sound of this fork brings healing.*[32]

## The corporate anointing, and the mantle of William Branham

On August 15, 2010, Bill Johnson and Kris Vallotton spoke at Bethel Church. Bill began the teaching with a sermon titled "The Real Jesus."

*"...Here's what I'm believing for – I know it's never happened; but I know that it must before the end. There must be, not just individuals – I'm thankful we have individuals that are rising up with such anointing, such strength, we have people scattered all over the planet right now that are just making a mess of things in all the right ways. We are so encouraged. But, what I'm believing for is a generation – a generation that'll rise up with a corporate faith, a corporate anointing to press into realms because it's my conviction that as much as God put on a William Branham, or a*

*Kathryn Kuhlman, or a Wigglesworth, He'll put far greater anointing on a company of people than He ever would on an individual.*[33] ***Video #30***

Then Kris Vallotton, Senior Associate Pastor at Bethel Church took over. He described for the congregation a conversation that he had with God about the entire church receiving the mantle of William Marion Branham:

> *...so, I was in a prayer chapel and laying on the floor and I said, "God, would you give me the mantle of William Branham?" And, He said, "Well, how could I do that? If I did that it would destroy you." Then, I was layin' there and it was like, the Lord asked 'how could I do that' so then I said – I waited about a few minutes – I was thinking about it and I said, "Well, you could put the same mantle on a whole generation—then we wouldn't stand out from one another." He said, "Alright, I'll do that."*
>
> *Isn't that awesome? That's what the Lord wants to do. He wants to put the, He wants – not just the mantle of William Branham, but how about the mantle of Jesus Christ? That's even a bigger one there, and, uh, He wants to put it on every single person.*[34]
> ***Video #30***

Many leaders in the New Apostolic Reformation including Johnson and Vallotton revere William Branham and admire him as a general of the Christian faith. But do their followers really know much about the man and his ministry? The following is a brief account:

William Branham lived from 1909 to 1965. He is known as the father of the Latter Rain/Charismatic Movements; the influence of whom many in the charismatic/Pentecostal churches are still operating in today. His meetings were the largest in America at the time. His ministry was, reportedly, one of the most dynamic, supernatural displays of healing that the church had ever seen. But along with the signs and wonders came a myriad of false doctrine and teaching, so much so that even his Pentecostal supporters became concerned and had mixed feelings about his ministry and about inviting Branham to their churches.

Some of the many false doctrines of Branham were: (1) the Trinity and church denominations are of the devil, (2) the three forms of God's Word are the Bible, the Zodiac, and the Egyptian pyramids, (3) his "Serpent Seed" doctrine which suggests that the serpent in the Garden had sexual intimacy with Eve that resulted in the conception of Cain, (4) his angel who taught him that he (Branham) was Elijah before the $2^{nd}$ coming as well as being the messenger of the last church age, Laodicea, (5) believers will reach immortality before Christ returns—and become a super race (also known as Joel's Army).

[An interesting side note is that Jim Jones, the founder and leader of People's Temple, who led thousands to suicide, was a follower of Branham and invited him to share a platform at Jones' church meetings in Indianapolis in June of 1956.]

In light of everything presented here about William Branham, one has to wonder why any minister/follower of the Lord Jesus Christ would be flattered to receive and/or pursue such a mantle from a man who was entrenched in the occult, and preached ideas so foreign and contrary to the Gospel of Jesus Christ—in spite of the "healing and miracle power" that he supposedly demonstrated.

## Conclusion
In case one has any doubts about what is happening at Bethel Church and what they aspire to, we conclude this section with the following information about a conference to be hosted at Bethel Redding led by John Crowder scheduled for February, 2020. On their website (thenewmystics.com), attenders are promised the following: *Video #28*

*Operate in trances, raptures and ecstatic prayer*
*Experience physical phenomena of mysticism*
*Get activated in creative miracles, signs and wonders*
*Understand and access new creation realities*
*Gain a historical grid of miracle workers and mystics*
*Be activated in the seer realm, prophesy, spirit travel*
*Receive open heavens and revelatory understanding*
*Access and manifest the glory realm*

WARNING! If the reader believes that the above subject matter of the Crowder conference is appealing, or you believe these practices are biblical, appropriate, and something Christians should be delving into, you are sadly deceived. You are playing with fire! [Also see *Video 29*]

Mixing Christianity with New Age practices not only goes against the Scriptures and waters down the gospel, but also opens up unsuspecting Christians to a world of mysticism, the occult and counterfeit spirituality. Although we, at Sound Word Ministry, believe that the gifts of the Spirit are still for today, we do not believe that mantles or gifts of dead people are "released" by God. Our God is the God of the living.

## Endnotes – New Age Fascination:

1.  Bill Johnson, *Dreaming with God,* Destiny Image Publishers, (Shippensburg, PA, 2006), p. 86
2.  Ray Yungen, *For Many Shall Come in My Name*, Lighthouse Trails Publishing, (Silverton, OR, 2007), p. 16
3.  Constance Cumbey, *The Hidden Dangers of the Rainbow*, Huntington House, Inc., (Shreveport, LA, 1983), p.54
4.  http://www.inspiredwalk.com/6297/alice-baileys-10-point-plan-to-destroy-christianity
5.  Judy Franklin and Ellyn Davis, *Physics of Heaven*, Double Portion Publishing, (Crossville, TN, 2012), Forward (Written by Kris Vallotton
6.  Ibid., p. 7
7.  Ibid., p. 14
8.  Ibid., p. 15
9.  Ibid., p. 18
10. Ibid., p. 164
11. Ibid., p. 169
12. YouTube, Shawn Bolz at Bethel Church https://www.youtube.com/watch?v=BU-oll6jO0Y **\*Video #4\***
13. Steven Bancarz and Josh Peck, *The Second Coming of the New Age*, Defender Publishing (Crane, MO, 2018, p. 18)
14. Ibid., p. 20
15. Michael G. Moriarty, *The New Charismatics*, Zondervan Publishing House, (Grand Rapids, MI, 1992), p. 271
16. https://www.nowtheendbegins.com/christalignment-bethel-church-using-satanic-destiny-reading-cards-deceive-followers-false-prophecies/
17. https://azusareport.com/christalignment-tarot-cards/
18. Ibid., the azuza report
19. https://store.theresadedmon.com/collections/clothing
20. https://www.youtube.com/watch?v=KioCOyhHgYM **\*Video #18\***
21. bssm-redding.blogspot.com
22. http://www.bethelredding.com/content/alabaster-prayer-house
23. http://bssm.net/schoolplanting/2016/09/20/how-to-lead-students-in-a-soaking-session/
24. *https://www.gotquestions.org/contemplative-prayer.html*
25. https://www.bibleguidance.co.za/Engarticles/Contemplation.htm
26. Op.cit., www.gotquestions.org
27. Yungen, Ray, *A Time of Departing,* Lighthouse Trails Publishing (Silverton, OR, 2006), p. 132

28. http://benij.org/.php
29. John Ankerberg & John Weldon, *Encyclopedia of New Age Beliefs,* Harvest House Publishers, (Eugene, OR, 1996), p. 26
30. http://www.benij.org/blog.php?id=1 *Video#6*
31. https://www.youtube.com/watch?v=Q25oPxQ7zHO&list=PL4NJjpnG33s8vt1KBM rHywctQZxUH13Y7   http://www.benij.org/blog.php?id=1*Video#7*
32. http://benijohnson.blogspot.com/ July 6, 2012
33. https://www.youtube.com/watch?v=vHcRI60jOHI&t=140s *Video 30*
34. https://www.youtube.com/watch?v=vHcRI60jOHI&t=140s *Video 30*

# V. Bethel School of Supernatural Ministry (BSSM)

> *Our mission is to equip and deploy revivalists who passionately pursue world-wide transformation in their God-given spheres of influence. Students are trained to continue in the ministry style of Jesus: to enjoy the presence of God, say what He is saying, and do what He is doing.*[1]—BSSM website

Bethel School of Supernatural Ministry (BSSM) is a one-to-three year school founded by Bethel Church in Redding, CA. It was started by Bill Johnson and Kris Vallotton in 1998 with 20 local students. The school has grown to a current enrollment of over 2400 with a representation of 70 countries from around the world. In 2017, the city of Redding approved a huge expansion project that will cost Bethel Church 96 million dollars to build a larger campus.

Bethel School of Supernatural Ministry is not the average Bible School for people to learn about Christianity and study the Bible. Students are taught how to "prophesy," and how to "activate" their supernatural gifts. But if gifts have to be taught and activated, are they really supernatural at all? On the online website, *Rooftops and Rafters,* BSSM is described like this:

> *The "prophetic lifestyle" dominates the whole perspective of the course—as it does in life generally in a Bethel culture—everything and anything comes from the need to operate in the realm of being prophetic. There are no boundaries for operating in the supernatural. Openly, course leaders will promote & expect risk taking, "stepping out" into God's glory or "all that God has for you." From what I have observed, it seems not to matter if there is no reference point in scripture. If there seems to*

81

*be a supernatural move of God or demonstration of his power, particularly in the miraculous, it is embraced fully and sometimes hunted/chased down. No manifestation "of the spirit" is enough—no encounter of God's glory too much. The watch-word is always "MORE".*[2]

Rick Becker in his online ministry, *Famine in the Land* article *Normalizing Mysticism* states that some people label Bethel as a cult—

*Some have compared it* [BSSM] *to Hogwarts, the School of Wizardry from J.K. Rowling's Harry Potter series. Bethel, itself, has been labelled a cult by others. What is certain, is that Bethel Church and their School of Supernatural Ministry are deceiving thousands of people all around the world.*[3]

They do not hide the fact that everything is "connected to the presence of God." This description on their website describes the school as follows:

*BSSM is a Holy Spirit-driven ministry school where students learn how to live in the Kingdom of God and extend its borders through a supernatural lifestyle. Everything is connected to the presence of God. We experience his presence when we gather together, and we learn that his presence follows us everywhere we go as we are transformed to be aware of it.*[4]

This description sounds very spiritual—very Christian. But what is the real meaning of the word "presence" as mentioned in the above description? Herescope Ministries in their online article, *The Passion of His Presence and the Purpose of the Passion* explains:

*Christ must come **to** His Church before He comes **for** His Church. They* [speaking specifically about The New Apostolic Reformation, emphasis ours] *believe there will be a separate "spirit" or "presence" infilling in the last days, evidenced with many signs and wonders. They say their passionate worship will invoke a "Presence" which will "energize the church with new power and demolish the works of Satan. This spirit of Christ (i.e., presence") will come first to indwell the church before Jesus' Second Coming.*[5]

Many discerning Christians believe that the "presence" experienced in the hyper-charismatic churches is a counterfeit, Gnostic Jesus and not the Jesus of the Bible. At Bethel School of Supernatural Ministry, one is introduced to this Jesus, and students are trained how to access, receive supernatural gifts from, and have an intimate relationship with this spirit. One does that through the laying on of hands to receive the "presence," soaking accompanied with contemplative prayer, and participating in hypnotic "worship" lasting for hours, to mention just a few ways.

You can see Bill Johnson first handedly "releasing the anointing" to his followers.
https://www.youtube.com/watch?v=dWeUNoR30_0&feature=youtu.be
*Video #8*

Students at Bethel School of Supernatural Ministry spend a good part of their training going out on the street to minister healing to the people in the city of Redding, California. They believe they receive words of knowledge in advance as to who to pray for and why before they go. This practice is called "treasure hunting." Many healings are claimed by BSSM students. Another way that they believe that they can receive this "presence" is by "grave sucking" described in the next section.

Some excellent videos to watch feature a defected student of Bethel School of Supernatural Ministry, Lindsay Davis, who gives her first-handed knowledge and reflection of the school and the movement, in general. *Videos #25 and #26* produced by Cultish Ministry https://www.youtube.com/watch?v=GF2t_VRorXQ]

## Grave Sucking

*There are anointings, mantles, revelations and mysteries that have lain unclaimed, literally where they were left because the generation that walked in them never passed them on. I believe it's possible for us to recover realms of anointing, realms of insight, realms of God that have been untended for decades simply by choosing to reclaim them and perpetuate them for future generations.* [6]—Bill Johnson

Probably the most bizarre activity coming out of Bethel School of Supernatural Ministry is the practice of "grave sucking," also known as "grave soaking." In 2013, many in the body of Christ were shocked and outraged as pictures appeared online (from Bethel's own Facebook posts) revealing BSSM students, along with Beni Johnson, lying on graves of dead, famous Christian faith healers such as: Smith Wigglesworth, Amy Temple McPherson, and Alexander Dowie, to name a few. They do the activity so that they can suck the anointing off of the dead bones buried in the graves. They believe that when people die, their anointing or "mantles" die with them; so that any unused portion or power still on them can be received by living believers as they lie on graves. They justify this practice using one single Bible verse in II Kings 13:21.

> *And it came to pass, as they were burying a man, that, behold, they spied a band of men; and they cast the man into the sepulcher of Elisha: and when the man was let down, and touched the bones of Elisha, he revived, and stood up on his feet.*

One time in the Scriptures, God worked this type of miracle in the Old Testament. It does not, by any stretch of the imagination, suggest that the man received any kind of gift or mantle or power from Elisha. God is the giver of gifts (Matthew 7:11), the anointing abides in us (I John 2:27); and there is nothing more that we have to do. Grave sucking is an outrageous, irrational, and despicable practice; and gives one of many examples of the deception the leaders and their followers are steeped in. "Grave sucking" is truly an abomination to God!

Grave sucking also demonstrates the focus of the followers of Bethel Church and the New Apostolic Reformation. It is one of many things they do to try to achieve "deeper levels" of the power that they think they need—even if strictly forbidden in the Bible. Christians are to have nothing to do with getting anything from the dead. The Lord makes it clear that touching anything dead is unclean (Numbers 19:16). There is never a reason whatsoever to go to anyone else but God, especially not to the dead, to receive any kind of power, gift or anointing. Sadly, it seems as if followers of Bethel Church and the NAR want the power gifts so badly that they are willing to go to such extremes. This is a very dangerous and demonic practice and makes most Christians cringe to even think about it. It is also a terrible witness to non-believers.

**Endnotes – Bethel School of Supernatural Ministry:**
1. BSSM website http://bssm.net/
2. https://rooftopsandrafters.wordpress.com/school-of-supernatural-ministry/
3. https://bcooper.wordpress.com/2018/04/16/bethel-school-of-supernatural-ministry-normalizing-mysticism-rick-becker/
4. BSSM website http://bssm.net/school/introduction/atmosphere/
5. http://ratherexposethem.blogspot.com/2014/04/herescope-passion-of-presence-purpose.html
6. Judy Franklin and Ellyn Davis, *The Physics of Heaven*, Double Portion Publishing, (Crossville, TN, 2012), p. 31

# VI. Other Things Bethel

## *The Passion Translation "Bible"*

In 2009, Brian Simmons claimed that Jesus Christ literally visited him in his room, breathed on him, commissioned him to write a new translation of the Bible, and gave him "the spirit of revelation." On Sid Roth's television program, *It's Supernatural*, Simmons described how *The Passion Translation* Bible (TPT) came about, and how he received a supernatural impartation for revelation.

> *Jesus came into my room, breathed on me, and then took me up to heaven. . . "He breathed on me so that I would do the project, and I felt downloads coming instantly. I received downloads. It was like, I got a chip put inside of me. I got a connection inside of me to hear him better, to understand the Scriptures better and hopefully to translate.*[1] **\*Video #16\***

Bill Johnson describes *The Passion Translation* as "one of the greatest things to happen with Bible translations in my lifetime,"[1a] however, many others disagree. On the *GotQuestions.org* website, we learn the following:

> *The Passion Translation is actually not a translation at all but is actually a Bible that has been re-worded and re-written, apparently intended to support a particular strain of theology. . . The Passion Translation of the Bible not only reflects Simmons'*

85

*New Apostolic Reformation (NAR) theology, but it appears to be deliberately written in order to promote it.*[2]

Holly Pivec, author, speaker and administrator of the online website, *Spirit of Error*, describes *The Passion Translation* as a way to re-word the Scriptures to fit NAR teachings and practices:

> *Simmons has taken verses of Scripture that have nothing to do with NAR teachings or practices and reworded them so they appear to support those very teachings and practices, such as "prophetic singing," the "transference of an anointing," and the issuing of "apostolic decrees." In other words, despite his claim to unveil the truth of the Bible "unfiltered by religious jargon," he's actually exploiting his audience's ignorance of sound textual criticism to smuggle in a heterodox theology along with a good measure of NAR jargon.*[3]

There are huge differences between the accepted translations of the Bible and *The Passion Translation*. By their own admission on *The Passion Translation* website, we learn about their value for actual, literal translation:

> *. . . The meaning of a passage took priority over the form of the original words. Sometimes in order to communicate the correct intended meaning, words need to be changed.*[4]

> *The Passion Translation is more in favor of prioritizing God's original message over the words' literal meaning*[5]

We learn more from the website, *GotQuestions.org* that Brian Simmons has changed and tampered with the original text of the Bible:

> *In other words, The Passion Translation of the Bible is not about finding corresponding words in different languages or presenting original words in a new language. The above comments imply that the Bible does not mean what it says, and so it needs to be changed to say what it should say. This is not an unfair assessment on our*

*part, as passages in The Passion Translation of the Bible show extreme tampering with the text.*[6]

Examples of tampering can be found here in Galatians 6:6:

*Nevertheless, the one who receives instruction in the word should share all good things with their instructor.* (New International Version)

*Let him who is taught the word share in all good things with him who teaches.* (New King James Version)

**And those who are taught the Word will receive an impartation from their teacher; a transference of anointing takes place between them.** *(THE PASSION TRANSLATION)*

It is clear that the NAR teaching of impartation—the belief that the anointing can be transferred from church leaders to church believers is evident in the translation of the above verse which has nothing to do with the original text. An example of adding to Scripture can be found in Luke 1:37:

*For nothing will be impossible with God. (New American Standard Bible)*

*For with God nothing shall be impossible. (King James Version)*

**No promise of God is empty of power, for with God there is no such thing as impossibility.** *(THE PASSION TRANSLATION)*

In addition, Brian Simmons went on to say on the same Sid Roth television program, *It's Supernatural,* that **while in heaven** he was taken to the library there. He said that he w*as* tempted to steal the book entitled, *John—Chapter 22* which, he reported, gives the mystery of the end-times, charismatic super-church. This is significant because the Gospel of John only contains 21 chapters. Simmons claims that "he will be given the information at a later date and then reveal it to the world. When he does, it will cause a worldwide spiritual awakening and make the name of Jesus famous." Don Pirozok talks about hidden knowledge reserved for the elite:

> This hidden knowledge which is available for only an adept privileged few is called "esoteric knowledge." In the movement which Simmons is declared to be an apostle, the push for "hidden esoteric knowledge is a huge factor." So prevalent is this belief, many prominent leaders make acclaim of heavenly visits, and communication with famous dead saints, or even speaking with angels. Often heavenly encounters also include "sitting on the lap of God," even though the Scriptures declare God dwells in unapproachable light. [7]

In an international, evangelical, peer-reviewed theological journal, Dr. Andrew Shead describes The Passion Translation as follows:

> ...abandoning all interest in textual accuracy, playing fast and loose with the original languages, and inserting so much new material into the text that it is at least 50% longer than the original. The result is a strongly sectarian translation that no longer counts as Scripture; by masquerading as a Bible it threatens to bind entire churches in thrall to a false god. [8]

In conclusion, Brian Simmons has reported that he received new revelation, and that God gave him special insight to translate the Bible. Holly Pivec, continues to point out the danger of this claim.

> But, for now, I want to point out that this translation is potentially one of the most disturbing developments in the NAR movement. Simmons is following in the footsteps of the major cults of Christianity who have released their own translations of the Bible, including the New World Translation used by the Jehovah's Witnesses and the Joseph Smith Translation used by some groups of Mormons. [9]

## Fire tunnels and the *Kundalini* Spirit.

A common practice at Bethel Church meetings and conferences are "fire tunnels." A fire tunnel is just one way they believe that the "anointing" is received. In a fire tunnel, expectant followers stand in line to receive what they perceive to be a "touch from God." They believe that this is a necessary practice for a believer to be continuously "filled up" with the Holy Spirit so that they will be "equipped" to get to the next level of their spiritual journey. Michael Boehm on his *Youth Apologetics Training* website, explains fire tunnels this way:

> *Believers line up in two lines and face inward, creating a tunnel and stretch out their arms inward. One believer walks through the tunnel as everyone yells "fire" repeatedly at them. The purpose is to fill them with "Holy Spirit." Often this leads to drunken-like behavior, uncontrollable laughter and violent jerking motions. Many people fall to the ground ("slain in the Spirit") after passing through the fire tunnel.[10]*

What exactly are these followers receiving as they proceed through the fire tunnels? Many Christians discern that it is the same spirit as the Hindu *Kundalini* spirit also known as the "serpent power." In Hindu meetings, devotees line up to receive a spiritual experience from a touch by an open hand, (mostly to the forehead) by the guru. After a while, the devotee begins to writhe, shake, jerk, scream, or laugh uncontrollably. These manifestations are called *kriyas*. **\*Video #8\*** (@10:01-10:36) https://www.youtube.com/watch?v=dWeUnoR30(Strom, 2010)

Fire tunnels became popular in 1994 when a movement began at the Toronto Airport Vineyard Church in Toronto, Canada called the Toronto Blessing (the church's name was later changed to Toronto Airport Christian Fellowship when they left the Vineyard Church). Believers came from all over the world to get a taste of this new "anointing" that can also be experienced at Bethel Church today. Mishel McCumber, in her book, *The View Beneath*, describes The Toronto Blessing as follows:

> *In this movement, the Holy Spirit was reduced to an alcoholic beverage that could entertain our senses and make us drunk. He became a commodity that could be poured out, passed around, transferred, imparted, and consumed. He became nothing more than an electrical current or an impersonal force that could be called down and directed to do man's bidding. In retrospect, this*

*movement denied both His personhood and His holiness. He became the organ grinder's monkey, tethered by a chain and commanded to perform. It was blasphemous![11]*

Having been to Toronto three times in the 90's, this author has to agree. I personally experienced the "anointing" for over twenty years after I attended services at Toronto, thinking I was receiving something wonderful from the Lord. I was deceived. I was experiencing what I believed, at the time, was valuable to my Christian walk. I not only received this experience personally but prayed for thousands of others to receive it, and also trained teams of people how to minister in it.

I cannot deny that the feeling was glorious. Coming out of the drug culture, it seemed very similar to intoxication only it was received by a touch on the forehead in the Name of the Lord Jesus Christ. I shook, rattled and rolled on the floor, and laughed for several hours at a time. There were times when I couldn't move as if I were stuck to the floor. I was addicted! I kept going back for more and more. I was led to believe that if I didn't keep receiving this "anointing," I would miss what God wanted to give me and, therefore, I would not be able to get to the "next level" in the kingdom.

It was really a difficult thing to come to the realization that something that seemed so right, so real, so glorious—was counterfeit! When I came to the knowledge of the truth, I never went back. I can honestly say that I am more content now that I know that I don't have to keep striving to receive the next "new thing" that God is supposedly "releasing." Mishel McCumber continues her description which supports my experience as well:

*. . . Once you were steeped in this atmosphere for a while, it was like taking a hit of spiritual heroin—you wanted more. There was something so persuasive, so enticing, so utterly addicting about it. It pulled you in and seduced your soul despite your questioning mind.[12]*

The Toronto Blessing allowed thousands of believers to experience a tangible "presence" of what they thought was God. While many leaders of the church were "drunk" and enjoyed the intoxication, there was nobody minding the fence. As a result, it opened the gates for the wolves to come in with a flood of false doctrines that is still happening today.

That's one reason why Paul told us to be alert and sober-minded—not drunk! On the christiantogether.net website, the following questions are asked about the *Kundalini*:

> *So what exactly are these 'manifestations' if they are seemingly at home in such an unholy environment? Are they from God at all? (I am talking here about the violent "jerking", uncontrollable laughter, bodily contortions, drunkenness, 'portals', strange "angel" encounters, etc.) Why do we not see such an 'anointing' in the Bible? Why aren't Jesus or the apostles promoting these manifestations if they really are true revival? Why instead do we see these things all the way through the New Age and Hinduism, etc.? Do we not realize that many false religions have their own version of "laying on of hands" that results in these very types of manifestations? This 'spirit' is not in the Bible - but it is all the way through Kundalini-type Hinduism! Don't you think this should alarm us?[13]*

Yes it certainly should alarm us and create big red flags in any Christian who is diligently a lover and seeker of truth. The quest for "more" goes back to the Garden of Eden. Adam and Eve had everything they wanted and needed. Yet apparently, it was not enough for them as they were still tempted by the serpent who told them that "they could be like God." That same lie is being perpetrated today in the hyper-charismatic church at large.

We see the *Kundalini* in operation on the followings video:
https://www.youtube.com/watch?v=HFKnsFwTrOl (PanteleAz, 2014) (@0:32 - 0:53) *Video #9*

On *Video #10*, you can see a comparison in the actions, behaviors and movements of people participating in a fire tunnel at Bethel Church, Redding, California as compared to Hindu ceremonies and gatherings which show the rattling signs of the *Kundalini* spirit: https://www.youtube.com/watch?v=V4R8jRDeEks (B, 2017)

No description of the *Kundalini* spirit emanating out of Bethel Redding, can be better understood than the one coming directly from a service at Bethel Redding with Heidi Baker speaking and releasing the "anointing": https://www.youtube.com/watch?v=vbEpJU1UMR0 *Video #11*

On *__Video 12__* (@ 0:36) you can see a disturbing display of a woman exhibiting *Kundalini* behavior all the while being ministered to with the Word of God. She appears to be in her own world—laughing, twitching, falling and spewing New Age doctrine to those around her. She is oblivious to the true gospel being quoted to her and laughs in the face of the street preacher: https://www.youtube.com/watch?v=6GQxMpcS1p8

### "Slain in the spirit"

Another part of the experience that goes along with the fire tunnels that you see at Bethel Church is the whole concept of being "slain in the spirit." It happens when supposedly the power of God comes upon followers—overpowering them physically, so much so that they can no longer stand up—causing them to fall (usually backward) into the arms of another church member called a "catcher." A "catcher" stands behind each one expecting this experience—waiting for the person in case they fall backwards, so he can lay the limp body down to the ground.

This experience happens after being touched usually on the forehead. Being "slain in the spirit" can also happen when someone shouts, waves their hands or blows on willing participants. The same manifestations then occur as the ones in the fire tunnels such as: shaking, convulsing, weeping, crawling, jerking, laughing and trance-like behavior. People who experience these manifestations believe that it is the Holy Spirit that comes upon them.

Proponents of the experience also say that it is a way for a believer to be refreshed and renewed, because they are empty and are in need to be "filled up" with more of God. They claim that being "slain in the spirit" can cause a wave of relaxation and euphoria. But this type of behavior does not line up with Paul's admonition as he expresses in two of his letters.

> *__Let all things be done decently and in order__* (when discussing the spiritual gifts practiced within the Christian fellowship.) I Corinthians 14:40

> *__That we may lead a tranquil and quiet life in all godliness and dignity.__* I Timothy 2:2

The word "drunk" doesn't appear anywhere in either verse. As a matter of fact, the word for *tranquil* in Greek is the word *eremos* (Strong's #2263).

It means *properly, placid, free from outward disturbance, without needless commotion, avoiding what is flamboyant or ostentatious* (biblehub.com)

Followers of Bethel and like-minded churches justify the experience biblically citing II Chronicles 5:13-14:

> *...and when they praised the Lord saying, "He is good for His lovingkindness is everlasting, then the house, the house of the LORD was filled with a cloud, so that the priests could not stand to minister because of the cloud, for the glory of the LORD filled the house of God.* [See also I Kings 8:10-11].

Nothing in the New Testament reports of such a happening except for when the soldiers fell backward when they came for Jesus in the Garden of Gethsemane. But these soldiers were not believers. In fact, they were enemies of Jesus, and obviously did not remain on the ground demonstrating strange manifestations. He did not impart anything to them, but instead, they continued to arrest Him.

Another justification for being "slain in the spirit" (and the manifestations that follow) is taught by leaders in the hyper-charismatic churches because they believe that Peter and the apostles were "drunk in the spirit" on the day of Pentecost. Yet when one examines the scripture in Acts 2:12-15, Peter specifically gives the explanation that they were **not drunk,** but that they only **appeared to be drunk** by the mockers in the crowd because they were speaking in different languages.

> *And they all continued in amazement and great perplexity, saying to one another, "What does this mean?" But others were mocking and saying, "They are full of sweet wine." But Peter, taking his stand with the eleven, raised his voice and declared to them: "Men of Judea and all you who live in Jerusalem, let this be known to you and give heed to my words. For these men are not drunk, as you suppose...*

Would Peter have been able to preach as eloquently as he did (Acts 2:14-41) if he were "drunk?" In fact, there are videos on-line where a speaker, Heidi Baker, (a friend of and frequent speaker at Bethel) is so under the power of this spirit—that she is not able to speak at all. To the contrary,

Peter tells us three times in his own epistle to "keep sober in spirit" [I Peter 1:13), "be of sound judgment and sober spirit for the purpose of prayer" (I Peter 4:7), and "Be of sober spirit, be on the alert." (I Peter 5:8).

Kevin Reeves in his book, *The Other Side of the River*, states:

> *Anything added to what God has already provided is a counterfeit. We don't need to get zapped, or experience extra-biblical manifestations in order to feel that we have arrived, or to earn inclusion into the mythical great end-times army of Dominion or Latter Rain doctrine.* [14]

Reeves continues to explain the dangers of being "slain in the spirit":

> *When folks get touched with this kind of power, they routinely become almost unteachable, preferring the experience to the Word of God. I can't relate how many times I've heard, "Well, maybe I can't find it in the Scriptures, but it happened to me, so it is real.* [15]

In summary, we believe that God is sovereign and there is a legitimate reason for a believer to become touched by the Holy Spirit in a powerful way. But certainly not as it is being experienced in a segment of the church today—people lining up for their next zap, seeking after thrills and being biblically illiterate, because it feels good and seems right. God wants us to be under the control of the Holy Spirit. Being filled with the Spirit means being humble and submissive to the authority of the Lord Jesus Christ—not drunk. "Slain in the spirit" or *Kundalini* spirit? Let the reader decide.

## Glory clouds/Gold dust/Feathers/and Jewels, O my!

During a service at Bethel Church, as onlookers stood in amazement, they alleged that a glory cloud strangely appeared that hovered over the ceiling of the building. There was a gold, glittery substance emanating from the so-called cloud that fell everywhere in the church.

You can actually see the event as it happened that night at Bethel at: https://www.youtube.com/watch?v=J21-fBgB44Q. (MastersPiece, 2015) *Video #13*

This explanation by Bill Johnson is taken from this same video:

*Why does He not show up in a way that He can be recognized? He told the Israelites, "I was in the cloud and I didn't let you see any form because I knew you to be an idolatrous people, and you would have created an idol after you created the image." He is not punishing us. He is wanting to give us as much as He can bless us and promote us without destroying us. And so it is happening tonight as the church is camping around the presence. We may not have an idea, a clue about what we are doing. And we certainly don't know what to do next. BUT FINALLY—THE MAIN THING HAS BECOME THE MAIN THING.* [16] **\*Video #17\***

In referring to the so-called glory cloud, "Finally, the main thing has become the main thing" is a very revealing statement. Is this really true for a believer in the Lord Jesus Christ that a so-called "glory cloud" is the main thing in his/her spiritual life? What about souls? What about living a sanctified life? We can learn more about the "glory cloud" from the description on the *GotQuestions.org* website:

*A physical manifestation of God's presence in the form of a glittery cloud that lingered over worship services. Such clouds have been reported in services all over the world, from one-room house churches in Brazil to megachurches in California. Those who have witnessed this phenomenon describe it as a glittering swarm of gold-like particles that settles on skin and hair and then vanishes upward. Some describe hands and faces covered in oil or a glittery residue that returns even after wiping it off. There are also reports of feathers or "jewels" falling from these clouds. Some pastors, usually in the Charismatic or Pentecostal movement, claim that the cloud has so enveloped them before preaching that they could hardly see the congregation. They attribute it to the tangible presence of God anointing them for preaching. They use as their biblical foundation Old Testament passages such as 2 Chronicles 5:14; 1 Kings 8:11; Ezekiel 10:4; and Exodus 40:35* [17]

Another good video to watch can be found on Todd Friel's *Wretched TV* website. Todd gives an excellent explanation which sheds some biblical light on what is happening with the "glory clouds" at Bethel Church: https://www.youtube.com/watch?v=5PvlW49FYBk (Vollrath, 2011).

You can also view the video on our playlist on our website – portions of which are transcribed here.

*Seeing but not believing... That was from the church of smoke and mirrors run by Pastor Bill Johnson in Redding California, part of the New Apostolic Reformation in cahoots with the IHOP movement in Kansas City, which has a third river flowing into this ocean of chaos, the Toronto Blessing. That supposedly was the glory of God coming down. That's one of the battle cry prayers of this movement: let the glory come around us, let the river—from the glory—of the heavens open up on the anointing—for the flowing of the glory—from the river..."*

*Well now, the glory supposedly is coming down, oddly enough, from the ventilation system and the kids are soaking it up. Let's consider for a moment the times that the glory of God has appeared before people. What happens to those people? Consider if you will, Moses. He had just seen a bunch of miracles by God and he said, basically, (I'm paraphrasing), "The miracles are great, but I want to see YOU, God!" and God said, "You can't see me because it would kill you!" So, instead, God's glory passed him by. Remember this analogy, not perfect, but pretty good. Anytime we see somebody in the Bible seeing the glory of God or even an angel, they FREAK out completely; totally scared and that's why God has to, that's right—totally scared. That's why God has to say, "Don't be afraid."[18] *Video #14\**

Glory clouds, feathers, angel dust, and jewels. How do these things get into the church services? Todd Friel continues with an explanation:

*There are two options that I can see: (1) caused by demons. They can do those tricks you know, or the other option that is actually worse, (2) caused by the preacher.[19] *Video #14\**

Furthermore, followers of the New Apostolic Reformation are told that the glory cloud is the *shekinah* glory now supposedly appearing in many of the hyper-charismatic churches worldwide. They also believe that there will come a time where His glory will be here permanently (on their elite group) as the manifested Christ on the earth before Jesus Christ returns. Some teach that this will be the second coming. But the Bible does not mention anywhere about a secret coming only to the elite. It does, however, tell us that "every eye will see Him."

"Slain in the spirit," fire tunnels, glory clouds, gold dust, gems and feathers—Are these the work of the Holy Spirit or the *Kundalini* spirit? Is the sole purpose of this phenomena an intent to distract a believer and/or usher in a "presence"—in this case being the supposed, manifest presence of God? We are in trouble when our feelings and/or experiences get in the way of God's Word.

> *An evil and adulterous generation seeks after a sign; and a sign will not be given it, except the sign of Jonah."* Matthew 16:4

## Jen Johnson and her blue genie (Black and White)

Brian and Jenn Johnson (Bill Johnson's son and daughter-in-law) are part of the senior team at Bethel. According to their website (brianandjennjohnson.com), "they are the co-founders of *Bethel Music, Worship U,* and have been integral in the production of over 15 albums that have influenced the culture of worship across the global church."

*Bethel Music was developed in 2009 to* "steward the songs coming out of Bethel and its worship leaders" (Bethel.com). On YouTube, you can find multiple pages of teachings by Jenn Johnson. One topic that is exceptionally disturbing and, at the very least profane, is the one called *Black and White.* Posted in 2011, the video is taken from a women's conference held in August of 2009. It is classic post-modernism at its worst. The full video remains on *Bethel TV* channel at the present time. https://www.youtube.com/watch?v=qdeqtJvkE5w&t=177s *Video #19*.

> *Not many of you should become teachers, my brothers, for you know that we who teach will be judged with greater strictness.* James 3:1

On the *Black and White* video, you can see Jenn Johnson asking the congregants to identify different words as either "black" or "white." She said that while spending time "soaking" on a friend's mountain, she knew her message would be about the subject of "black and white," and the Lord told her to ask Him about the gray scale.

She claims that when she googled how many shades of gray there are, the response was "This question is yet to be answered." (This writer did not find that to be the case when the same question was googled.) Ultimately she opined that if you don't allow God to define the gray areas, someone else will define them for you. Her teaching was not easy to follow as she spoke in vague, inexact concepts and platitudes. The following is a portion of the teaching:

> *But there is a gray scale of emotion that He carries. And joy can be black for you and joy can be white for you but there is not one answer. And I looked up the word "gray scale" and it defined black and white as this. Black and white are exclusively composed of shades of gray. And the only way the gray is defined is because of how the light is shown through the color. The only way we can know the answer for the specific situation is by letting His light specifically for your situation shine through.* [20] **\*Video #19\***

It is surprising to think about the fact that she did not mention the Word of God at all in her message. Is she implying that there are no absolutes, when in fact, as Christians, the Bible IS our absolute? This came across to this writer as a way to influence a congregation to believe that with God—there is a gray area. When one begins to receive teaching like this, it is a slippery slope because anything goes, and anything becomes acceptable. This leads to what is acceptable to the person instead of using the Bible as the standard to know what is acceptable to Him and what is not. This is exactly what is happening in the hyper-charismatic church today—anything goes!

But her description of the Holy Spirit and the actions of the angels as they circled the throne are even more alarming. On any given Sunday, multitudes of churches are worshipping to *Bethel Music*. While Brian and Jenn are "stewarding" the music and songwriters, where is their oversight, and who is stewarding Jenn Johnson? Think of that as you read the following:

> *"God, Jesus, Holy Spirit, I can't define who He is to you. You need to ask Him to define Himself to you. I feel like I'm supposed to ask you to ask Him some questions today. And I want you to go to Him and ask Him to define who He is to you and what that looks like. So God to me, Jesus to me, the Holy Spirit to me **is like the genie from Aladdin.** That's black you might say. I don't care. **That's who He is to me.** He's funny, **He's sneaky** He's silly, He's wonderful. He's like the wind. He is all around.* [emphasis ours]

98

*You know the scene in Revelation where the angels circle the throne? And they say, "Holy," and it's this reverent like holy. Every time they circle the throne, they see a new side of His face and they're just taken aback. It's all they can do to say, "Holy". They just keep circling because there's never an end. It's limitless to what they see as they circle. And I was thinking yesterday, I thought, I wonder how much they laugh because He's funny. I wonder how much He goes, "look at this" and they're like, "ha ha." What part of happy isn't reverent? I'm just asking, I don't know. I thought of those angels circling the throne, and I thought, I bet they text each other. I bet they have farting contests. That is black, get her off the stage! That is irreverent! God's a heck of a lot more fun than we think He is. It doesn't take away from the value of absolutely being awestruck to the point of being speechless before a creator.*[21]

After hearing this kind of speaking, it should have caused any sincere seeker of Christ to get up and leave. But it appears that the people in the congregation thought the things Jen Johnson was saying were really funny. She is obviously blind to the misrepresentations she makes. The Holy Spirit is just that—HOLY, and not a genie which is defined as—"a spirit of Arabian folklore as traditionally depicted imprisoned within a bottle or oil lamp, and capable of granting wishes when summoned."

> *For the time will come when they will not endure sound doctrine; but after their own lusts shall they heap to themselves teachers, having itching ears;* II Timothy 4:3

The fact that the video described above is still available to view—is almost as disturbing as the video itself. Is there not one leader at Bethel who would take a stand, denounce the content and remove this blatantly profane video?

In October of 2016 on *The Line of Fire* program, Dr. Michael Brown questioned Bill Johnson regarding Jenn Johnson's "blue genie" comments. The following is Johnson's response:

*First of all, I'm not going to defend because that is language I wouldn't use. She talks about the Holy Spirit being sneaky and He is. He is mysterious. And I think that's accurate. I wouldn't use that terminology, and she doesn't use it anymore. She hasn't for years; because it was honest on her part to try to explain what she was experiencing with God which is very, very real and genuine. The language that was used, she would never use again because it caused such controversy in a wrong sense. Well I don't mean controversy but, in a way, that might misrepresent the Lord, and she doesn't want to do that. I don't want to do that. But yes, she has used descriptions like that for sure. I've seen them, and I've had good conversation with her about it.*[22] ***Video #20***

Bill Johnson goes on to say:

*. . . that sometimes in our somewhat humorous culture we have crossed the line although mostly I think it's well intentioned. In fact, in her case, I know it is.*[23] ***Video #20***

The issue of the angels' actions around the Throne of God in Jen Johnson's video was not brought up on *The Line of Fire* program. In any event, no matter which color, the following Scripture is a huge contrast to Jenn Johnson's irreverent portrayal of the actions of angels:

**And all the angels were standing around the throne and around the elders and the four living creatures; and they fell on their faces before the throne and worshiped God, saying, "Amen! Blessing and glory and wisdom and thanksgiving and honor and power and might, be to our God forever and ever. Amen.** Revelation 7:11-12

## Todd Bentley Commissioning Service

Todd Bentley, a Canadian evangelist, found worldwide fame in 2008 in what was known as the "Lakeland Revival" in Lakeland, Florida. He originally planned to speak for just a few days, but ended up conducting dozens of revival meetings, and stayed there for several months.

Many healings were claimed (though no medical evidence has been forthcoming) in the course of these meetings. The bizarre "manifestations of the spirit" drew much attention—including Bentley's tendency to punch and kick sick people seeking prayer: https://www.youtube.com/watch?v=RL6muB_FGEE ***Video #15***

It wasn't long before the elite (the "apostles") of the New Apostolic Reformation, including Bethel's Bill Johnson, came along to put their stamp of approval on this supposed "move of God," publicly prophesying over Bentley (and about Bentley) and the so-called "revival." But what does the Bible say about prophecy?

> *But the prophet who presumes to speak a word in my name that I have not commanded him to speak, or who speaks in the name of other gods, that same prophet shall die. And if you say in your heart, 'How may we know the word that the Lord has not spoken?' When a prophet speaks in the name of the Lord, if the word does not come to pass or come true, that is a word that the Lord has not spoken; the prophet has spoken it presumptuously. You need not be afraid of him.*
> Deuteronomy 18:20-22 ESV

Given the number and severity of the warnings in Scripture for us to be on our guard against false prophets (Jeremiah 23:16, Luke 6:26, Matthew 7:15-20, Matthew 24:24, 2 Timothy 4:3-4, 1 John 4:1 to mention just a few), it would be extremely unwise for us to assume that everyone who claims to speak for God is a prophet or has spiritual insight—and is, indeed, operating in a prophetic gift from God.

We can see from the above Scripture in Deuteronomy that one of the simplest ways (though not the only way) to tell who is a true prophet and who is a false prophet—is whether or not the things prophesied actually happen. The prescribed standard is not revoked or watered down in either the Old or New Testaments. In spite of that, the prevailing teaching regarding prophecy and prophetic gifts in the hyper-charismatic church today is that a true prophet can prophesy falsely and still be considered a true prophet—a notion which, of course, has no biblical support.

With this black and white biblical standard in mind, let us examine some portions of what was said (by the top leaders of the NAR "apostles" and "prophets" including Bill Johnson) about Todd Bentley and the Lakeland Revival on and around the occasion of Bentley's commissioning, "apostolic alignment" ceremony.

But please keep in mind, as you read the following "prophesies," that within weeks after the commissioning service (and the glowing remarks that were "prophesied" about Bentley by these "apostles/prophets"), it was later revealed that Bentley was having an affair with his intern/children's nanny while these "revival" services were happening, and at the time frame that the commissioning service was taking place.

**C. Peter Wagner (founder and chief "apostle" of the NAR and who conducted the proceedings):** *I take the apostolic authority that God has given me, and I decree to Todd Bentley—your power will increase, your authority will increase, your favor will increase, your influence will increase, and your revelation will increase. I also decree, that a new supernatural strength will flow through this ministry; a new life force will penetrate this move of God. Government will be established to set things in their proper order.* ***God will pour out a higher level of discernment to distinguish truth from error.*** *New relationships will surface to open the gates for the future!*

**Che Ahn (NAR apostle):** *I want to proceed in recognizing that God has chosen you [Todd Bentley] and appointed you to bear much and lasting fruit in this Lakeland Revival and revival around the world. Recognizing that He has called you as an Ephesians 4 evangelist and revivalist moving in signs and wonders. Knowing that you have walked in a manner worthy of the Lord,* ***pleasing Jesus in every way, bearing fruit in every good work****, and growing in the intimacy and knowledge of God.*

**John Arnott (pastor of Toronto Airport Christian Church):** *We bless you today, Todd Bentley. You're a friend,* ***you're a man of God, you're a man of prayer, you're a man of the spirit.*** *You love the anointing. And I would say that it's not just the Lakeland Revival, but the whole world that goes into revival. And you're leading an amazing charge, and multitudes are getting in behind you and saying, "Come on, I'm gonna go with you." And so we bless all of that. Thank you, Holy Spirit, for raising up this young man to lead such a mighty charge around the world.*

**Bill Johnson (pastor of Bethel Church):** *We shape the course of history by partnering with you [Todd Bentley], giving honor where it's due.* ***You welcome the glory as well as anybody I've ever seen in my life. I long to learn from you in that.*** *And I bless you, and I pray with the rest of these that the measure of glory would increase. That Moses would no longer be* *considered the high-water mark where the glory shone from his face, but instead the revelation of the goodness of God would change the face of the Church. And that He would use your voice, He would use your grace, your anointing to alter the face of the Church before this world. That the goodness of the Lord would be seen once again. I pray this over you in Jesus Name.*

**Stacy Campbell**: *When we were singing that song tonight, the spirit came on me and said 'Todd, because you asked, like very few men on the face of the earth, ask to see my glory—I will begin a revival through you that will pass beyond gifts into the very heart that moves God to release gifts to his children....Todd, I've chosen you because of your background, to release My nature when you release My gifts—to become a living epistle like the word that became flesh and people saw the glory of God. And I will use you to father a movement that operates in such revival power when it is coming out of the very nature and heart of God. And you will teach people how to behold God until they are transformed from glory to glory, from compassion to mercy to lovingkindness, to truth, to justice, to forgiveness....I feel like Todd that when you were 12 years old, and I just graduated from Baptist seminary, the Holy Spirit fell on me, and He started to speak to me over and over and over again about a generation that would come on the earth, that would do signs and wonders, that would change society, and society would not change them, and you are a first fruits of that generation of nation changers that will release the glory of God in all its fullness in Jesus' name.*[24]

There was much more said by several other prominent "apostles" and "prophets" in the course of the ceremony. You can watch more of the commissioning service on our website. **\*Video #21\*** and **\*Video #22\***.

All very encouraging words from men and women reputed to be apostolic and prophetic pillars of the modern church, but **all completely empty and false in the light of day**. As noted, it is public knowledge that within weeks of this "apostolic alignment" commissioning service, Todd Bentley was exposed as an adulterer and drunkard, and he stood down from ministry. It is sad to say that even after many pleas from his own peers, Bentley proceeded to leave his wife and three young children to marry his children's nanny.

Rick Joyner, along with Bill Johnson were overseers of Todd Bentley's ministry "restoration" process. They reinstated him back in ministry after a very short time. Many leaders in the body of Christ disagreed with the decision of the restoration team because some thought there hadn't been enough time for Todd Bentley to be "restored," and some thought that he should not be in ministry again. In August, 2019, more allegations of extreme sexual misconduct with many different victims were brought about by a man associated with Bentley's ministry. The claims were about activities Bentley was engaged in up to the present time—most of which he has denied.

As great as the prophetic words and declarations sounded when Bentley was commissioned, every one of them failed the test of Deuteronomy 18:20-22 and, therefore, those who spoke them were shown to be false prophets. There is no biblical way around it, and yet while there were admissions of having been deceived, there are yet to be public confessions of false prophecy given by any of the commissioning "apostles."

Curiously, and what should have been the most obvious red flag is that Bentley, earlier in his ministry, claimed that God told him directly **NOT to preach Christ, but to preach—angels!** Bentley explains his supposed conversation with God:

> *You know, I told the Lord, "Why can't I just move in healing and forget talking about all that—other stuff?"*
> *He said, "Because, Todd, you gotta get the people to believe in the angel."*
> *I said, "God, why do I want people to believe in the angel, isn't it about getting the people to believe in Jesus?"*
> *He [God] said, "The people already believe in Jesus, but the church doesn't believe in the supernatural.* [25] *****Video #23*****

Todd Bentley claims that he has had several angelic visitations. That in itself isn't alien to biblical experience as there are a number of accounts in the Bible reporting angels visiting human beings for specific purposes. However, we are also told in Galatians 1:8 that "even if we or an angel from heaven should preach to you a gospel contrary to the one we preached to you, let him be accursed."

One must also seriously consider whether Bentley's ongoing ministry is set on a firm biblical foundation or flights of fancy. Are his claims of direct revelations from God true, or is he lying? Or does he himself genuinely believe them, but their origins are either demonic or the outpourings of a delusional mind? So clearly, even if these visitations were real, we must examine their content and fruit. Only a fool would believe the words of an angel over the Word of God! Todd Bentley describes another one of his "angelic" visitations:

> *Later, the Lord began to show me the purposes behind these visitations at different times in my life. When the angel visited me on December 5th in Grant's Pass, I was knocked out of my body and had an out-of-body experience like the Apostle Paul did. It was, at that time, that the word of knowledge increased in my life.*

> *There has been an increase in my accuracy and frequency of delivering the word of knowledge since that visitation. All of a sudden, I began to experience more open visions, more trances and more seer/prophet stuff in which my eyes would be open to the invisible realm and what was going on in the realm of angels and demons.*

> *Through different prophetic ministry friends, I have since come to understand that I received a real deposit of that same kind of revelatory gift that God placed upon William Branham years ago. It was only after that visitation that I was able to touch people with my left hand and accurately diagnose their sicknesses. This is the same kind of gift that William Branham [inaudible word] during the Voice of Healing Revival exactly 50 years before.* [26]

So in the course of these visitations and through "prophetic" ministry, Bentley claims that the Lord showed him that he had been gifted in the same way that William Branham had been years ago. Yet, as you read earlier in this book, William Branham had a fascination with the occult and also spoke against the Holy Trinity—and preached a false Christ and a false gospel. We can, therefore, safely surmise that whatever these angelic visitations were, they were NOT from the true and living God. This, in turn, further demonstrates a lack of even a basic level of biblical discernment on the part of those involved in Bentley's commissioning service, including Bill Johnson who continues to endorse and promote Todd Bentley's ministry to this day.

105

In reflecting on Todd Bentley and the Lakeland Revival, one can't help be reminded of the account God gives us in I Kings 22:19-23:

> *Micaiah said, 'Therefore, hear the word of the LORD. I saw the LORD sitting on His throne, and all the host of heaven standing by Him on His right and on His left. The LORD said, 'Who will entice Ahab to go up and fall at Ramoth-gilead?' And one said this while another said that. Then a spirit came forward and stood before the LORD and said, 'I will entice him.' The LORD said to him, 'How?' And he said, 'I will go out and be a deceiving spirit in the mouth of all his prophets.' Then He said, 'You are to entice him and also prevail. Go and do so.' Now therefore, behold, the LORD has put a deceiving spirit in the mouth of all these your prophets; and the LORD has proclaimed disaster against you.*

## Sozo

Followers of Bethel Church are encouraged to participate in *Sozo*—their controversial ministry of inner healing and deliverance. It has become extremely popular in a large segment of the church, and is spreading rapidly worldwide including but not limited to such countries as: Czechoslavakia, South Africa, Russia, Nicaragua, Singapore and Australia. The word, *Sozo*, is a Greek word that means saved, made whole, and delivered. The word, *Sozo*, appears in the Book of Matthew alone sixteen times for diverse reasons. Some examples are as follows:

> *She will bear a Son; and you shall call His Name Jesus; for He will <u>save</u> His people from their sins.* Matthew 1:21

> *And they came to Him and woke Him, saying, <u>Save</u> us, Lord; we are perishing!"* Matthew 8:25

> *For the Son of Man has come to <u>save</u> that which was lost.* Matthew 18:11

> *But the one who endures to the end, he will be <u>saved.</u>* Matthew 24:13

*For she said within herself, If I may touch His garment, I shall be whole.* Matthew 9:21

We learn from these Scriptures that the word, *Sozo,* describes how Jesus gives us forgiveness for our sins, protects us from danger, heals our diseases, and promises to help us in the tribulation that is to come. But we learn from *GotQuestions.org,* a synopsis of Bethel's application of *Sozo* and how the *Sozo* ministry is administered there and beyond:

*A Sozo session is designed to provide Holy Spirit-led wholeness and freedom for the Sozoee (the one seeking deliverance). Sozo requires the presence of a mediator or guide who is trained to walk Sozoees through a time of prayer and reflection that is supposed to facilitate intimacy with God. The facilitator guides the Sozoee through an ascent of the "Father Ladder," in which the Sozoee is encouraged to "visualize" God and speak to the image of the Lord created in the mind's eye. This is followed by identifying various "doors" that have allowed sin to enter one's life, closing them, and "sealing" them by the blood of Jesus. Obstacles to the process are identified as "walls" that must be torn down. When a "door" is closed or a "wall" is demolished, the Sozoee is told to give a single clap of the hands, supposedly to help disengage the lie that had taken root in his or her mind. Past hurts are explored as various "rooms" of the mind are opened and searched—Sozo practitioners even claim to track down spiritual wounds acquired in the womb! Of course, none of this is found in Scripture.*[27]

We are never told to visualize anything in the Bible. In fact, visualizing is very dangerous especially where past memories and relationships are concerned. Berean Research Ministry, in their online article, *Sozo, a Dangerous Inner Healing and Deliverance Ministry* tells us why:

*Today we easily find mysticism, false teaching, divination, abuse of spiritual gifts, and love of experience trumping the Word of God. When you fall into this area the problem is that the spirit world will deliver.* **Those seeking to be in the "presence of Jesus" will indeed find themselves in the company of an entity but it will not be the Jesus of the Bible.** *Remember that "Satan himself masquerades as an angel of light.* 2 Corinthians 11:14.[28] [emphasis ours]

Another reason that *Sozo* is so injurious to Christians is that there are accounts that can be found on-line from people who have had extremely negative experiences, and have been alienated from family members because of false memories that surface during *Sozo* sessions. The following is a testimony of an associate of our ministry who personally participated in a Sozo session. [used by permission]

> *I had Sozo ministry in 2011. I was already familiar with most of the terminology and the methods involved. I had been through some of the training to become a Sozo practitioner, so it didn't seem especially weird to me at the time. In retrospect, I can now see how bogus and dangerous Sozo ministry is! Some of the major issues I see from my personal experience are: 1) the implantation of **false memories**, and the havoc they can wreak, 2) the **false diagnosis** of problems and 3) the giving of **false hope** for things that God has not promised (but the Sozoee is led to believe He has).*
>
> *For me, the false memories and the false diagnosis above happened in tandem. I was, at the time, on the receiving end of an abusive marriage. My now former spouse subjected me to just about every category of abuse over many years, but I had generally blamed myself and/or accepted it as how my spouse showed love. However, before the Sozo session, the abuse had been getting worse. I decided to open up about it during the session and disclose a small part of what had been happening. I kept the details vague—and said that my spouse was frequently very angry, extremely critical and put me down a lot. Having just disclosed that, the Sozoer said a prayer to ask "Holy Spirit" to bring forth a memory. He then asked me what had come into my mind.*
>
> *I answered that I had the image of my mother looking angry. I was then led, via suggestion and further "revelations" (supposedly from God), to accept that my spouse was, in fact, NOT abusive in the ways I'd described. In fact, I was led to believe that I was projecting my mother's abuse that I experienced in my childhood onto my spouse; and had unfairly filtered my spouse's words and behavior towards me through this lens. I was subsequently led through a series of prayers of forgiveness towards my mother and repentance for believing "lies" about my spouse.*

108

*I was left with "memories" of my mother being abusive and a renewed attitude of acceptance and submission to the ever-increasing abuse from my spouse. The truth, however, was the polar opposite of what was "revealed" in this Sozo session! My mother was and remains an amazing, loving, patient, generous woman who was NEVER abusive to me or any of my siblings. I thank God that I quickly realized that the scandalous accusations levelled against her by the Sozo practitioners were utterly false.*

*At the same time, rather than being offered help to escape the abuse I was actually experiencing at home, I was effectively silenced from speaking out about the abuse (after all, how could I speak out and seek help about something that "Holy Spirit" has revealed wasn't real?) and led to believe it wasn't really happening. I sort of knew the accusations against my mother weren't true, but these people speak as if they are the authority of God. So what was I supposed to make of it, and how could I effectively discern? Surely if God were speaking through a prophetic ministry like Sozo, then who are we, as mere mortals, to question that—even though our best knowledge and all the evidence is to the complete contrary, and we have no ACTUAL memories of the things "revealed?"*

*As it turned out, before my spouse and I finally separated around 18 months later, I was subjected to an escalation of the abuse— all of which I internalized and took the blame for. It got to the point that after the divorce, I had a total mental collapse followed by years of panic attacks, massive anxiety, depression, suicidal thoughts and required treatment by specialist PTSD therapists. But I sarcastically ask, "How could this be, if "Holy Spirit" revealed I wasn't really being abused?"*

*The 3rd major point is the false hope one receives in Sozo ministry. I'd had some very specific and very hard to attain career aspirations for many years. About five years before the Sozo ministry, I had finally laid these aspirations to rest and was happy to have moved on. However, during the Sozo session, perhaps inevitably, the subject of "dead dreams" came up. To make a long story short, I left the Sozo session fully convinced that I was FINALLY being given what I'd spent years striving for—which renewed false hope in me. Yet seven years later, none of what I was supposedly "shown" has materialized—not even remotely. The raising of false hopes is a cruel trick of the NAR, designed to keep one beholden to the "prophetic ministry" for the next steps towards your dreams—when really it's just a carrot on a stick and yet another recipe for potential mental anguish and the shipwrecking of one's faith.*

Thankfully, the person in the above testimony has overcome much of the adversities of life and is a strong believer today—but not because of Sozo. In fact, Sozo just heaped even more to work through and made things much worse due to the false memories that were presented as truth. Even though well intended, it is apparent that the "revelation" that this person received was not coming from God yet declared in the name of Jesus Christ.

This is just one of the major reasons the ministry is so dangerous and causes us to want to warn people against it. For some Sozo recipients, they receive the opposite of what is promised by Sozo: "to be better able to walk in the destiny that they have been called." Some final thoughts about Sozo.

*The experience-based, extra-biblical practices of Sozo are of human invention and require human instruction—not to mention the payment of a "suggested donation." With its visualization techniques, guided meditation, and "soaking prayer," Sozo is, in many ways, closer to New Age mysticism than to Christianity.*[29]

### Endnotes – Other Things Bethel:

1. https://www.youtube.com/watch?v=1nTFcsSlFvM&t=73s **Video #16***
1a https://www.thepassiontranslation.com/about/endorsements/
2. https://www.gotquestions.org/Passion-Translation.html
3. Holly Pivec, Spirit of Error website http://www.spiritoferror.org/2013/04/a-new-nar-bible-the-passion-translation/3014
4. https://www.the passiontranslation.com/about/endorsements/
5. https://www.the passiontranslation.com/about/endorsements/
6. https://www.gotquestions.org/Passion-Translation.html
7. Don Pirozok, Association of Charismatic Evangelicals https://www.facebook.com/acemembers/posts/1815608762077818
8. https://www.alisachilders.com/blog/heres-why-christians-should-be-concerned-about-the-passion-translation-of-the-bible Bethel Church and Christianity.
9. http://www.spiritoferror.org/2013/04/a-new-nar-bible-the-passion-translation/3014

10. Michael Boehm, *Youth Apologetics Training*
    http://youthapologeticstraining.com/bill-johnson-exposed-08-portals-spirit-travel-sozo-and-angel-orbs/
11. Mishel McCumber, *The View Beneath*, Mighty Roar Books, (Canada,2016), p. 41
12. Ibid, p. 42
13. https://www.christianstogether.net/Articles/209364/Christians Together in/Survival Kit/Kundalini spirits in.aspx
14. Kevin Reeves, The Other Side of the River, Lighthouse Trails Publishing, (Eureka, Montana, 2007), p. 83
15. Ibid., p. 84
16. https://www.youtube.com/watch?v=lvjMPccZR2Y *Video #17*
17. https://www.gotquestions.org/glory-cloud.html
18. https://www.youtube.com/watch?v=ie_p_EOF_CU *Video #14*
19. Ibid., https://www.youtube.com/watch?v=ie_p_EOF_CU *Video #14*
20. YouTube, Bethel TV, Published 5/21/11, Black and White https://www.youtube.com/watch?v=qdeqtJvkE5w&t=142s *Video #19*
21. Ibid., https://www.youtube.com/watch?v=qdeqtJvkE5w&t=169s *Video #19*
22. Michael Brown, *Line of Fire Ministry* https://www.youtube.com/watch?v=Af1hswGOjZg&feature=youtu.be *Video #20*
23. Ibid., https://www.youtube.com/watch?v=Af1hswGOjZg&feature=youtu.be *Video #20*
24. Part 1: https://www.youtube.com/watch?v=w4YlqSV949g *Video #21*
    Part 2: https://www.youtube.com/watch?v=QmuNHHEvgZs *Video #22*
25. https://www.youtube.com/watch?v=yr6_SjrasFQ *Video #23*
26. Todd Bentley, Fresh Fire Ministry http://www.freshfireusa.com/writings/view/174-MY-PERSONAL-JOURNEY-INTO-THE-HEALING-MINISTRY-Part-3
27. https://www.gotquestions.org/Sozo-prayer.html.
28. https://bereanresearch.org/sozo-a-dangerous-inner-healing-and-deliverance-ministry/
29. https://www.gotquestions.org/Sozo-prayer.html

# VII. *Bethel Music/Jesus Culture*

Bethel Church is one of the main leaders of a worldwide movement carrying incredible momentum which continues to grow enormously. One of the explanations for their rapid growth is through the music group, *Jesus Culture* band.

We have heard it said that *Jesus Culture* music is the "gateway drug to the supernatural." Another has described *Jesus Culture* music as "Hansel

111

and Gretel's crumbs" that is used by Bethel as a way to lure and indoctrinate unsuspecting people, especially youth, into the New Apostolic Reformation's cesspool of deception.

The group is not only meant to produce music but to promote revival, and to teach the theology and practices of Bethel Church such as: tangible spiritual encounters with God by "igniting an awakening," and turning believers on to a "presence" that they believe is important to experience God's love and power. Not only is their goal to change the church but also to change the world via their music and spiritual agenda.

## What is *Jesus Culture*?
On the *Jesus Culture* website, the question is asked, "What is Jesus Culture?"

> *Jesus Culture is a community of worship leaders and musicians whose heart is to see a generation **impacted by encounters with the presence of God**. Jesus Culture is focused on equipping a generation to **transform society by bringing people into an encounter with God's love through worship** and discipleship. The songs they release capture the heart of the movement.*[1] [emphasis ours. Please note that Jesus Christ or the gospel is not mentioned anywhere to describe what *Jesus Culture* is.]

Also on the *Jesus Culture* website, the question is asked, "What is the future for Jesus Culture?"

> *Our highest ambition is to continue releasing music that **brings people into encounters with God**. We also hope to encourage young worship leaders who desire to write the songs of revival and use anointed music **to ignite an awakening**. Our plan is to propagate worship leaders by cultivating them at **a deeper level** through training and discipleship. As a ministry, we want to **create an atmosphere** for song writing as we develop young emerging artists—the future voice of a generation.*[2] [emphasis ours]

As you can see, the word "encounter" is mentioned several times. A serious concern is their emphasis of experience over doctrine. The following is an excerpt from Wikipedia voicing concerns about *Jesus Culture*:

*Indeed, Jesus Culture is sometimes criticized for a lack of depth and biblical teaching at their conferences and concerts. The emphasis is on having an undefined "personal encounter with the love of God" rather than on repentance and faith. Such an emphasis appeals to emotion, and as with anything centered primarily on emotion, those participating often miss the mark. Any time we give preeminence to emotional experience over the clear teaching of the Word, we open the door to potentially harmful doctrines.*[3]

### Music that bypasses the intellect

Jesus Culture music is pleasing to the ear and carries incredible musical excellence. However, *Jesus Culture* music can be trance-like and even hypnotic when sung over and over—sometimes the same chorus twenty or more times. With that in mind, it is understandable why Bill Johnson would make the following revelatory statements:

*Music bypasses all the intellectual barriers, and when the anointing of God is on a song, people will begin to believe things they wouldn't believe through teaching.*[4]

*As the atmosphere changes, as encounters become more alive, suddenly we find ourselves thinking differently.*[5]

Can statements be any more revealing as to how important music is to this movement, and why the two cannot be separated? Johnson's statement is a tacit admission to the fact that *Bethel Music* and *Jesus Culture* use music to bypass people's God-given intelligence and discernment.

The question is why? Why would a Christian ministry want to lead its listeners to a place where their intellect is bypassed, and are caused to believe things they wouldn't normally believe (except through the Holy Spirit's leading and the teaching of the Word of God)? This is a very slippery slope and leaves true followers of Jesus Christ vulnerable to be deceived—one of the very things that the Lord Jesus Christ warned us about.

How else could leaders of a movement possibly lead thousands of sincere, Bible believing Christians to turn off their minds, and place feeling and encounters over sound doctrine while, at the same time, lead them to participate in forbidden practices of the occult and New Age? By Johnson's own statements, he answers the question. It is by the influence of their music, false prophetic, extra-biblical revelation and the addictive, feel good experiences of the "anointing" that causes thousands to be deceived.

### Jesus is my "boyfriend."

Some of *Jesus Culture* music reflects very intimate, "Jesus is my boyfriend," provocative-type lyrics. One example is a song entitled, *How He Loves Us* written by John Mark McMillan/Bethel Music. Some excerpts of this song are as follows:

> *He is jealous for me. Loves like a hurricane, and I am a tree. Bending beneath the weight of His wind and mercy. When all of a sudden, I am unaware of these afflictions eclipsed by glory, I realize just how beautiful you are and how great your affections are for me.*

> *We are His portion and He is our prize. Drawn to redemption by the grace in his eyes. If grace is an ocean, we're all sinking (ha ha). So heaven meets earth like a sloppy wet kiss. And my heart turns violently inside of my chest. I don't have time to maintain these regrets when I think about the way. He loves us. . .*

Another Bethel Music song is *The More I Seek You* written by Zack Neese/Gateway Create Publishing. Some of the lyrics are as follows:

> *I want to sit at your feet. Drink from the cup in your hand. Lay back against you and breathe. Feel your heart beat. This love is so deep. It's more that I can stand. I melt in your peace. It's overwhelming.*

*Another song by Bethel Music is entitled Laid Down Lovers sung by Nikki Mathis:*

*I want to be a laid down lover. So I lay down for you. I don't want to be half-hearted. Lord I want to burn for you.*

## Burning for Jesus

What does it mean to "burn for Jesus"? Could it be an explanation about burning that we get from popular teacher and friend of Bill Johnson, Mike Bickel, who explains on his website the "spirit of burning" and what it means to have a "passionate desire for Jesus"?

*"Spirit of burning" – This is a cycle of maintaining a passionate desire for Jesus so that you are in a place of emotional pain whenever he is absent; hope and excited expectancy because of the real experiential encounters with His beauty and presence causing you to have an even greater, intense desire to be close to Jesus.* [6]

*We have to get people beyond dedication and into fascination.* [7]

**"For there are certain men crept in unawares, who were before of old ordained to this condemnation, ungodly men, turning the grace of our God into lasciviousness, and denying the only Lord God, and our Lord Jesus Christ."** Jude 4 (KJV) [The definition of lasciviousness: inclined to lustfulness, wanton, lewd, arousing sexual desire, indicating sexual desire or experience of lust.]

Mike Bickel wrote a book called, *Passion for Jesus*. His teachings on the Song of Solomon are highly respected and embraced by the hyper-charismatic church, and is reflected in some of the lyrics of *Jesus Culture* music. *Herescope* online ministry describes Mike Bickel and his interpretation of intimacy as follows:

*Passion for spiritual experiences of the highest level is what Bickel is after through his spiritual interpretation of Scripture. Their Jesus is an imposter and the spiritual experiences are not "intimacy with God" but spiritual fornication.*

*. . . This IHOP "spirit of burning" concept is missing in scripture because Jesus IS absent and will be absent until He*

*returns again. This "spirit of burning" is simply a description of a deep lust for spiritual experiences and a spiritualizing of 1 Co 7:9.[8]*

At a *Jesus Culture* concert, *Jesus Culture* singer, Kim Walker-Smith sang the song, How He Loves Us, and ended the song by telling young people repeatedly that they need a love encounter with Jesus and their lives will never be the same after they do. Here is a sampling of what Walker-Smith spoke that night:

> *His presence. His love. Is so thick and tangible in this room tonight. There are some in this room who have not encountered the love of God. And tonight God wants to encounter you. He wants you to feel His love, His amazing love. Without it, these are just songs, these are just words, these are just instruments. Without the love of God, it's just like we're just up here making noise. But the love of God changes us, and we're never the same. . . His love is going deep tonight. . . See the Father. Behold the Father. Behold the Father (ha)[8A]*

This is yet another way to imply that "just" playing instruments and "just" singing to worship God, just because He is our wonderful God is not enough. She is subtly indoctrinating the minds of young people that they need to experience His love tangibly, and that they are able to get something from Him while worshipping.

### Reckless Love of God?

On another note, one of the most popular songs by *Bethel Music* is called *Reckless Love of God*. It was written by Caleb Culver, Cory Asbury, and Ran Jackson. Needless to say, the song has caused controversy in the body of Christ. The chorus is as follows:

> *Oh, the overwhelming, never-ending, **reckless love of God** Oh, it chases me down, fights 'til I'm found, leaves the ninety-nine. I couldn't earn it, and I don't deserve it, still, You give Yourself away. Oh, the overwhelming, never-ending, **reckless love of God**, yeah.*

The song is very melodious and pleasant to the ear, and used for worship in churches everywhere. But, on the other hand, the phrase "reckless love of God" is very disturbing to many believers because they feel very strongly, that in no way, shape, or form is God's love ever "reckless." The word "reckless" is often referred to as the activities of irresponsible drivers, criminals and/or those exhibiting rebellious, inappropriate behavior and one who makes poor choices—not our Almighty, Creator of heaven and earth. In fact, the word "reckless" is never used in a way to describe anything good, pure, or holy. Most dictionaries define the word "reckless" as:

Utterly unconcerned about consequences; rash, careless, impetuous.[9]

Many Christians disagree with equating God's love as being utterly unconcerned about consequences or being careless. In addition, as believers in the Lord Jesus Christ, the phrase "reckless love of God" is downright offensive and irreverent—partly because it was out of His love for us that He was willing to endure the cross—the very opposite of being reckless. God knew the consequences—a very deliberate plan as a way to redeem mankind.

In Georgi Boorman's, thefederalist.com article, *Sorry Bethel, God's Love is Not Reckless* (December 28, 2018), she makes the following points about "reckless love":

*To sing of God's "reckless love" is to downplay his omnipotence and sovereignty in favor of a weaker, more vulnerable and "approachable" version of him. All too often, worship lyrics map the attributes of man onto God instead of promoting a more biblical understanding of him. We seek to package his attributes in concepts we are already familiar with, instead of acquainting ourselves with the God who reveals himself through the Scriptures. We bring God down to our level, instead of seeking to understand him on his own terms.*

*As worshippers, we are obligated to ask ourselves: do the words coming out of my mouth, which are supposed to guide us in worshipping God for who he really is, accurately reflect God's character? If they don't, then how can we be worshipping in "spirit and truth?" (John 4:24)*

Boorman goes on to caution worship leaders to be careful stewards of the lyrics they present to the flock and the responsibility that the lyrics carry:

*Songs have tremendous power to influence our thought. We are vulnerable and emotional during worship, trusting the people leading us through the set, so church leaders must be careful stewards of the lyrics they present to the flock. If a particular lyric is promoting a less biblical understanding of God's character, as "reckless love" clearly is, then it needs to be corrected. Sheer popularity cannot override that imperative.*

When asked about the phrase, "reckless love of God," one of the writers, Cory Asbury, attempts to offer the following as his explanation and justification.

*"When I used the phrase, 'the reckless love of God,' when we say it, we're not saying that God Himself is reckless, He's not crazy. We are, however, saying that the way He loves, is in many regards, quite so. But what I mean is this: He's utterly unconcerned with the consequences of His own actions with regard to His own safety, comfort and well-being. He doesn't wonder what He'll gain or lose by putting Himself on the line, He simply puts Himself out there on the off-chance that you and I might look back at Him and give Him that love in return."[10]*

The question is—Is one able to separate the nature of God from the love of God considering that GOD IS LOVE? Love is at the very core of who God is. So for many believers, the answer is "No!" Furthermore, Asbury's explanation, no matter how he tries to explain it, does not justify using the word, "reckless" to describe anything pertaining to God—especially His wonderful love. The meaning of the two words, "reckless" and "God" are as far as the east is from the west. It's just not a match, not a fit. There are many words that can be used to describe the love of God, but it makes no sense to use "reckless" as one of them. Simply put, it is just not true!

But what does the Bible say about "reckless?" It appears in the New Testament in II Timothy 3:4 (NASB). It is used to describe one of many words identifying the unholy behavior of those in the last days:

> *But realize this, that in the last days difficult times will come. For men will be lovers of self, lovers of money, boastful, arrogant, revilers, disobedient to parents, ungrateful, unholy, unloving, irreconcilable, malicious gossips, without self-control, brutal, haters of good, treacherous, reckless, conceited, lovers of pleasure rather than lovers of God, holding to a form of godliness, although they have denied His power. Avoid such men as these!*

In the Old Testament, we can find the word "reckless" in Jeremiah 23:31-32. God uses the word not to describe Himself. On the contrary, He is speaking of how He feels about false prophets:

> *Behold, I am against the prophets, declares the LORD, "who use their tongues and declare, 'The Lord declares.' Behold, I am against those who have prophesied false dreams," declares the LORD, "and related them and led My people astray by their falsehoods and reckless boasting; yet I did not send them or command them, nor do they furnish this people the slightest benefit," declares the Lord.*

Once more in Zephaniah 3: 4-5, the word "reckless" is used to describe false prophets but then in the next verse—describes God as the opposite.

> *Her prophets are reckless, treacherous men; her priests have profaned the sanctuary. They have done violence to the law.*
> *The LORD is righteous within her; He will do no injustice.*

There are some who say that "reckless" is only a word and people who are offended by singing it in a worship song are being too ridiculous and petty. But words mean something! And in light of the above Scriptures, one has to agree that "reckless" is an inappropriate word to ever describe

God, yet can appropriately be used, as the Bible does, to describe aberrant humans and/or false prophets.

### Banning Liebscher

The founder and leader of *Jesus Culture* band is Banning Liebscher. Liebscher wrote a book titled, *Jesus Culture*. He writes this about his vision:

> *My vision is to see the Church demonstrating the Kingdom of God by engaging people with the raw power and radical love of God. This is what possesses me – and this is the remnant I am called to help raise up.*[11]

If anyone reading this book still has any doubt that *Jesus Culture* is just about nice worship music and nothing more—you can clearly see from Liebscher's own admission what exactly *Jesus Culture* is about in the following statements by him:

> *. . . to help raise up a generation upon whom the **glory** of the Lord has risen and to whom the nations will come.*[12] [emphasis ours]

> *God is releasing healing revivalists again across the earth, and my mandate is to help raise up and release them.*[13]

What is the "glory" that Banning Liebscher talks about? In a book written by Abraham Rajah (which he calls an apostolic and prophetic dictionary), he describes the word, "glory" like this:

> *The Glory may also speak about a certain **dimension** or level where God's **presence** can be witnessed or sensed. This sort of **atmosphere** is often referred to as **open heaven**. When the glory of God is **manifested** signs such as silver and gold dust, angels, angel feathers, heavenly manna, smoke, clouds, oil, creative miracles, etc. can be seen. The Shekinah glory refers to the visible presence of God's glory which is usually seen in a cloud of smoke (Ex. 16:7; Isa 40; Hab 2:14). **Going from glory to glory** refers to the increase of the glory dimension operating or present in the life of a believer. Every believer is called by God to **ascend** into **new levels of glory** (2Cor. 3:18)*[14] [NAR buzz words emphasis ours—see p. 9].

International Bible teacher and founder of Moriel Ministries, Jacob Prasch, powerfully makes the following comparison between the New Apostolic Reformation and hexachlorophene as to how this movement is affecting young people. He starts by explaining "that thirty years ago, it was seen as harmless to humans in diluted amounts. Now we know it is a more serious toxin that can kill and be particularly lethal to children."[15]

> *Hexachlorophene is not an innocuous compound that achieves 'good' as many thought. It is a dangerous one that only appears to achieve 'good' at the expense of very serious harm. Its bio-chemical impact is physiologically noxious and hazardous to the young especially. The NAR is exactly the same. It is spiritually and theologically noxious and its consequences are particularly detrimental to the young believers whom wolves like Wagner, Bill Johnson, Bickel, and Joyner like to target. As with Hillsong in Australia, it is the young people who get hurt first and worst.[16]*

In light of the fact that the proponents of NAR claim that blowing shofars, waving flags, Strategic Level Spiritual Warfare (the expelling of demons off of buildings and nations), and creating certain sounds through worship (just to name a few examples), when done in the name of Jesus, can deliver us from demonic oppression—Prasch's statement about how hexachlorophene, at one time, was considered a good way to kill germs — is especially profound. Prasch continues:

> *There were pharmaceutical research chemists and specialist consultant physicians—experts in toxicology who blew the whistle on hexachlorophene. The average user did not understand it as 'bad' because it seemed to 'kill germs.' The NAR is much the same. The average Christian just does not have the means to understand it. It seems good.[17]*

## Conclusion
Many churches worldwide regard worship as a way to reach the younger generation. They use worship as a way of entertainment so that people will be drawn into coming to church. But as we sing praises unto the Lord, it is important to be mindful of what we are singing to our God and Father.

We know that many people who listen to *Jesus Culture* music are committed believers in Jesus Christ. Yet when one is informed about the beliefs and practices of Bethel Church and the New Apostolic Reformation, every believer needs to ask the following question—is it possible to separate the music and mission of *Jesus Culture* from the ministry and messages of Bill Johnson and Bethel Church? The words of Jesus in Matthew 7:18-20 answers that question for us:

> *So every good tree bears good fruit, but the bad tree bears bad fruit. A good tree cannot produce bad fruit, nor can a bad tree produce good fruit. Every tree that does not bear good fruit is cut down and thrown into the fire. So then, you will know them by their fruits.* Matthew 7:18-20

The following was posted on the Ferocious Truth Ministry Facebook page: [9/2/19 by Zack Knotts].

> *Church leaders only endorse the music of Bethel Church for one of two reasons: Willful ignorance or willful agreement.*

If you are a pastor or worship leader reading this book and are using *Bethel Music* in your worship services—could this be a stumbling block for someone in your church? That through worshipping to songs from *Bethel Music* or the *Jesus Culture* band in church, a young person might be indoctrinated by the false doctrines of Bethel Church as outlined in this book. Remember the words of Jesus Christ when he says:

> *But whoever causes one of these little ones who believe in Me to stumble, it would be better for him to have a heavy millstone hung around his neck, and to be drowned in the depth of the sea. Woe to the world because of its stumbling blocks! For it is inevitable that stumbling blocks come; but woe to that person through whom the stumbling blocks come.* Matthew 18:6-7

What is a stumbling block? From the Biblehub.com, we learn that the word for stumbling block in Greek is *skandalon* (Strong's 4625) which means:

*A stick for bait (of a trap); generally a snare, an offense; the mechanism closing a trap down on the unsuspecting victim; an impediment placed in the way and causing one to stumble and fall.*

We pray that the reader will truly seek the Lord in prayer about these important questions. And also if you are a worship leader or pastor, we pray that you will truly see how much of a responsibility that you have to protect your sheep from the wolves and avoid the danger of anything that could cause someone to stumble or be devoured.

## Endnotes – Jesus Culture:

1. https://jesusculture.com/music/
2. https://jesusculture.com/music/
3. https://en.wikipedia.org/wiki/Jesus_Culture
4. https://bethelmusic.com/blog/bill-johnson-quotes/
5. https://bethelmusic.com/blog/bill-johnson-quotes/
6. Herescope, Mike Bickel's Gigolo Jesus, May 1, 2008 http://herescope.blogspot.com/2008/05/mike-bickles-gigolo-jesus.html
7. https://jesusculture.com/posts/1564-the-spirit-of-burning/ Accessed 3/16/2019
8. https://herescope.blogspot.com/2014/03/bridal-eschatology.html
8a. https://www.azlyrics.com/lyrics/jesusculture/howheloves.html
9. *Webster's Universal College Dictionary*, Gramercy Books, (New York, 1997), p. 659
10. https://churchfront.com/blog-churchfront/2017/11/8/reckless-love-by-cory-asbury-song-meaning-review-and-worship-leading-tips
11. Banning Liebsher, *Jesus Culture,* Destiny Image Publishers, Inc., (Shippensburg, PA, 2009), p. 32
12. Ibid., p. 43
13. Ibid., p. 44
14. Abraham S Rajah, *Apostolic & Prophetic Dictionary*, West Bow Press, (Bloomington, IN, 2013), p. 45
15. https://www.moriel.org/component/k2/item/1789-the-new-apostolic-reformation-nar-hexachlorophene.html?fbclid=IwAR18CUZGg4_F34lHF5NlET0pT386LCIDqriqOgNa Wz9pClaZyfa84_yP1eY
16. Ibid.
17. Ibid.

# VIII. Special Contribution
## A pastor's message to the church
### Rick Becker, South Africa

I graduated from high school in 1981, and went directly into the South African Air Force to complete two years of national service. But the only work that I wanted to pursue, and believed I was called to—was the ministry. After my two years in the defense force, I spent four years at a Bible college, followed by a year at *Youth with a Mission* (YWAM) abroad. I was married in 1992 and, shortly afterward, received a call to be one of the pastors at a small church in our city.

I was responsible for the youth, ran a home group Bible study, and preached on some Sundays. A few months later, our lead pastor came back from a visit to the USA, and reported to us that he had received an "increase in his anointing." Shortly thereafter, we saw visible changes in the way meetings were conducted. After the sermon, the chairs were moved to the side of the hall, and this became the time for "the spirit to move."

During these times there were prophecies, and the lead pastor would blow on people as he ministered to them. Although not as bizarre as what we witness today in NAR circles, my wife and I became increasingly uncomfortable with what was taking place.

A "prophetess" in the church regularly saw angels, visions, and the focus was on these kinds of encounters with God. One day we were in her home with a few others for a prayer meeting. By this stage, I believe people had noticed that I was skeptical of what was deemed the next "move of the Holy Spirit." The prophetess came up to me and began to shake me violently. This was supposed to be symbolic of God wanting me to wake up to what He was doing. The prophetess told me that I had to unconditionally accept this "move of God." My wife and I could not continue in this environment anymore.

The last sermon I gave was on deception in the church, and I resigned shortly afterwards. We moved to a different city, and received a letter from the same "prophetess" who told us that my wife would no longer be able to have children, and our pantry would remain bare until we repented.

This was my exit from charismania and the early stages of the New Apostolic Reformation. A new season dawned for me, and the best way is to describe it is—a wilderness. There was no internet in South Africa at that time. All I had were the Scriptures, a *Matthew Henry Commentary*, a few A.W. Tozer books, and my books from Bible college. Through many trials and tribulations, through searching the Scriptures, and by the grace of God, my eyes were opened even further to the aberrant teachings and practices of charismania and the New Apostolic Reformation.

## The cost of leaving.

There is a cost involved for members and especially those in leadership when coming to a crossroads of this kind. I was committed to serve the Lord full-time. I had prepared myself through obtaining a degree in theology, and there was nothing else that interested me.

I had a choice to make. I could stay in the ministry, and follow my inner conviction; or more importantly, leave because the practices taking place could not be supported by the Scriptures. Perhaps there are folks reading this who are at a similar crossroads. Maybe you think that you stand to lose too much if you leave. The opposite is true. You stand to lose much by participating in any ministry that has swerved from the truth, and is deceiving people. Keep in mind that teachers will be held to a stricter judgement.

> *Not many of you should become teachers, my brothers, for you know that we who teach will be judged with greater strictness.* James 3:1

Stepping down from a ministry usually means a loss of income, friendships and fellowship. Ultimately, if God has opened your eyes to any form of false teaching that is happening in a church or a ministry that you are part of—you have no choice but to address the issues. If there is no acknowledgement on behalf of the leadership that their teachings are contrary to sound doctrine followed by repentance—you have to leave!

For many years, my wife and I could not find a church fellowship. I went through a period where I regretted my time in Bible college. I saw it as wasted years, and wondered why I once believed I had a call to ministry.

125

I had received many flattering prophecies during my time at church, and now everything I had envisioned for my future lay in tatters.

The disappointment was really a result of my past, man-centered theology being shattered. I was no longer as important as I had thought. God was going to fulfill his purposes on the earth and in the church without me! This sobering truth is the complete opposite than what is taught in the NAR. **The emphasis is not on what Christ has done, but on what we can do.**

**Some contrary beliefs about NAR are:**

> *God needs us to usher in his kingdom.*
>
> *We become partners with God.*
>
> *We perform greater miracles than Jesus.*
>
> *We receive crucial revelations.*
>
> *We decree and declare.*
>
> *We decide our destiny.*

This kind of man-centered theology appeals to the flesh. It's one of the reasons so few are able to break free from this insidious movement.

**How the NAR infiltrates churches, and what to look out for.**
In a world where the large majority of the visible church are biblically illiterate, it's relatively easy to grow a church and sustain a "successful" ministry. In South Africa, churches across the nation from large cities to small towns have been influenced by the teachings of the NAR.

NAR teachings come into a church through offered courses, Bible studies, teaching materials, and the effective Trojan horse being —worship music. *Jesus Culture* and *Hillsong* **music are the gateway to the teachings of these two movements.** Once they can capture your emotions, your heart overrides your mind. Critical thinking is replaced with trust in the leadership who, after all, are "hearing from God" regarding the new direction that particular church is taking.

In South Africa, many folk in the ministry have taken on the title of "apostle" or "prophet." The title alone gives the impression that these people are something special—closer to God than ordinary believers with the ability to receive direct revelation from Him. Unfortunately, they go from bad to worse.

Soon leaders will find it necessary to attend a Bethel or a Hillsong conference, and then new materials and courses such as Sozo or a school of supernatural ministry will be introduced. Members will observe new terminology coming from the pulpit. The following catch phrases are a means by which we can identify NAR teachings: "shift," "heaven on earth," "apostles and prophets," "alignment," "presence," "atmosphere," "impartation," "seven mountains," "download," "activation," and "acceleration" just to name a few.

**A hallmark of New Apostolic Reformation churches is that they:**

Teach topically, using proof texts to substantiate their false doctrines.

Employ eisegesis (they ignore the rules of interpretation and original meaning of the text). Instead, they subject it to their own interpretation, and narcigesis (a self-centered interpretation of a text).

Relate experiences and tell stories which are usually not verifiable and are contrary to the Scriptures. God's word is ignored or twisted beyond its original meaning, resulting in progressive error.

*While evil people and impostors will go on from bad to worse, deceiving and being deceived. But as for you, continue in what you have learned and have firmly believed, knowing from whom you learned it and how from childhood you have been acquainted with the sacred writings, which are able to make you wise for salvation through faith in Christ Jesus.*

*All Scripture is breathed out by God and profitable for teaching, for reproof, for correction, and for training in righteousness, that the man of God may be complete, equipped for every good work.* 2 Timothy 3:14-17

127

When the word of God is neglected, something else will creep in and take its place. When a church starts focusing on spiritual experiences and encounters, you can know for certain that it is on a dangerous path.

**CAUTION:** Compelling stories, promises of intimacy with God, the lure of being a part of a new breed, and signs and wonders are captivating naïve folk across the globe.

**CAUTION:** People supposedly take trips to heaven, receive downloads, new revelations, and new interpretations of Scripture.

A church that has been influenced by the NAR will minimize the gospel when it comes to evangelism. The power shifts from the gospel, to the supernatural demonstrations of men and women. This concept can be traced back as far as 1985, when John Wimber released his book, *Power Evangelism*.

The NAR teaches that an encounter with God, or supernatural demonstration is crucial in order to convert believers. To the contrary, Scripture states that power is in the gospel, not signs and wonders —

> *For I am not ashamed of the gospel, for it is the power of God for salvation to everyone who believes to the Jew first and also to the Greek.* Romans 1:16

An experience never takes precedence over the Word of God:

> *But even if we or an angel from heaven should preach to you a gospel contrary to the one we preached to you, let him be accursed.* Galatians 1:8

The rich man in Hades thought that if his five living brothers had the experience of someone returning from the dead to preach to them, they would repent.

> *Abraham replied: "If they do not hear Moses and the Prophets, neither will they be convinced if someone should rise from the dead.* Luke 16:31

Jesus knew that signs alone, were not sufficient to save the lost.

*Now when he was in Jerusalem at the Passover Feast, many believed in his name when they saw the signs that he was doing. But Jesus on his part did not entrust himself to them, because he knew all people.* John 2:23-24

## A few reasons why people don't leave the New Apostolic Reformation:

1. **Someone may say, "I play a valuable role in the church, I simply cannot leave."** This is all the more reason for you to leave, especially if you are in leadership. You may be the secretary, lead the worship, teach a bible study group or, as in my case, even be one of the pastors.

You might think you will let people down, and the thought of leaving can cause a sense of guilt and betrayal. This is when you need to step back, and examine the situation in the light of God's Word, as well as from an eternal perspective.

When you leave a church that teaches false doctrine, you are playing a valuable role! Your actions alone will be a powerful testimony. You have made a stand for the faith and you are refusing to betray the Word of God. It is better to be guilty in the eyes of carnal men and women, than to stand before God and give an account for compromise.

Many are false converts. Don't expect false converts to see the light when they are firmly entrenched in the kingdom of darkness and loving it. When Jesus said, "My sheep hear My voice," He did not mean He will give you a new revelation during your quiet time. He meant true believers will hear and obey His voice. His voice is clear, His voice has spoken. It's called Scripture. These false converts need the true gospel in order to repent and believe, before they can be able to discern the errors of the New Apostolic Reformation.

*The natural person does not accept the things of the Spirit of God, for they are folly to him, and he is not able to understand them because they are spiritually discerned"* 1 Cor. 2:14

129

Don't think for a second that many caught up in these movements are not passionate or sincere, yet they are sincerely wrong. **Passion, crowds, testimonies, and even signs and wonders do not guarantee that God is involved.** Ultimately, God knows who are His, and what may fool men—never fools God!

> *Not everyone who says to me, "Lord, Lord," will enter the kingdom of heaven, but the one who does the will of my Father who is in heaven. On that day many will say to me, 'Lord, Lord, did we not prophesy in your name, and cast out demons in your name, and do many mighty works in your name?' And then will I declare to them, 'I never knew you; depart from me, you workers of lawlessness.*
> Matthew 7:21-23

2. **Many are simply feeding their own passions** and are getting exactly what they desire—ear tickling messages. It's not so much a question of them being deceived by a teacher, but rather them finding a teacher who is as deceived as they are. It's hard to believe the message of the cross over a message that avoids the cross and elevates self. We are quick to blame false teachers who are leading many astray, but these verses give us the reason many are deceived.

> *For the time is coming when people will not endure sound teaching, but having itching ears they will accumulate for themselves teachers to suit their own passions, and will turn away from listening to the truth and wander off into myths."* 2 Timothy 4:3-4

Note the following from the above Scripture:

The people will not want sound doctrine.

The people already have itching ears.

The people are the ones accumulating false teachers.

The people are merely catering for their own carnal passion.

The people are not interested in the truth.

The prophets of the Old Testament also had to contend not only with false prophets, but also with a people who preferred to satisfy their passions rather than to obey God.

*An appalling and horrible thing has happened in the land: the prophets prophesy falsely, and the priests rule at their direction; my people love to have it so, but what will you do when the end comes?* Jeremiah 5:30-31

*For they are a rebellious people, lying children, children unwilling to hear the instruction of the Lord; who say to the seers, "Do not see," and to the prophets, "Do not prophesy to us what is right; speak to us smooth things, prophesy illusions, leave the way, turn aside from the path, let us hear no more about the Holy One of Israel.* Isaiah 30:9-11

Don't be fooled by those in these movements, who by outward appearances seem to be devoted to God and His kingdom. They seem so passionate and determined to make a difference in this world—they are bold, unashamed, and eager to spread their message. Dig a little deeper however, and you will find that ultimately they are the ones who are exalted. It's a man-centered gospel with its leaders making statements such as:

You will leave a legacy.

You will usher in God's kingdom.

You will do greater things.

You will be a world changer.

God needs you.

3. **Some believe they can simply ignore the bad teaching—eat the meat and spit out the bones.** To put it another way—"Don't throw the baby out with the bathwater." There is no biblical mandate for this argument. Those who teach contrary to the gospel need to be marked and avoided, not marked and ignored.

*Now I beseech you, brethren, mark them which cause divisions and offences contrary to the doctrine which ye have learned; and avoid them.* " Romans 16:17

In his letter to Timothy, Paul explains that someone approved by God "rightly divides the word of truth." (2 Timothy 2:15). He then gives an example of two teachers who did not rightly divide God's Word: "Hymenaeus and Philetus, who have swerved from the truth, saying that the resurrection has already happened. They are upsetting the faith of some." (2 Timothy 2:18)

Finally, Paul tells us what our response should be:

*"But God's firm foundation stands, bearing this seal, "The Lord knows those who are His," and, "Let everyone who names the name of the Lord depart from iniquity."* 2 Timothy 2:19

By sitting under a pastor who twists the Word of God, you are submitting yourself to someone God has disqualified, and submitting yourself to someone who is responsible for damaging the faith of their followers. Your pastor should, in fact, be the one rebuking those who teach false doctrine.

[He] *"Must hold firm to the trustworthy word as taught, so that he may be able to give instruction in sound doctrine and also to rebuke those who contradict it"* Titus 1:9

The church at Thyatira was rebuked for *"tolerating that woman, Jezebel, who calls herself a prophetess and is teaching and seducing my servants."* Revelation 2:20.

We must avoid the irreverent babble of those who distort the Word of God to suit their own carnal appetites. False teachers need to be silenced, not supported:

*For there are many who are insubordinate, empty talkers and deceivers, especially those of the circumcision party. They must be silenced, since they are upsetting whole families by teaching for shameful gain what they ought not to teach"* Titus 1:10-11

4. **Some say that despite false teachings, God still moves.** We need to clarify what "God still moves" actually means. By this argument, people are usually referring to signs and wonders, testimonies from people in the church, or perhaps their own experience. I'm sure you have heard similar expressions such as these: 1) "the presence of the Lord was so strong during the service," or 2) "there was such a powerful anointing during the meeting and Holy Spirit was present."

**CAUTION! When subjective experiences take precedence over the Word of God, we are dealing with mysticism—not biblical Christianity!** People falling over backwards, gold dust appearing during services, rain falling during an outdoor prayer meeting, fire tunnels, goosebumps during worship, and even signs and wonders are not evidence of God moving. These last days will include many signs and wonders, but they won't be a result of God moving—but of deception.

*For false Christs and false prophets will arise and perform great signs and wonders, so as to lead astray, if possible, even the elect.* Matthew 24:24

*The coming of the lawless one is by the activity of Satan with all power and false signs and wonders, and with all wicked deception for those who are perishing, because they refused to love the truth and so be saved. Therefore God sends them a strong delusion, so that they may believe what is false, in order that all may be condemned who did not believe the truth but had pleasure in unrighteousness."* II Thessalonians 2:9-11

5. **Pride prevents many from admitting their whole house has been built on the wrong foundation.** It's embarrassing to admit that much of what you have believed, practiced and, (in the case of pastors), taught others has been based on a lie. I can sympathize with pastors who have fallen for the lies of the NAR and then have their eyes opened to the deception.

The question you must ask is this: "Am I prepared to stand before God and be numbered with those who have taught a false gospel, a different Jesus, and promoted a different spirit?"

**Run from this deception! Inherent in this movement is the dependence on people and experiences instead of God.** A typical NAR service is no dull affair. Lively worship with *Hillsong* or *Jesus Culture* music can stir up emotions. Gold dust, glory clouds, angel sightings, and fantastic stories of encounters with God leave followers drooling in their seats. After the message, it is time for the "spirit to move" and prophecies are given. People are "slain in the spirit," impartations and declarations seal the deal.

But now that you have left, there is silence. What stirred your soul is gone, and you wonder if a dry alternative is all that God has to offer. What you may not yet have realized is that **the "more" that you were seeking was actually poison.** People who live on junk food and a high sugar diet live in a state of toxic hunger. They are perpetually hungry because their bodies are not being fed the nutrients that they are so desperately craving and needing. Instead they keep giving their bodies what they think it wants, rather than what it truly needs.

In the same way, people who are fed on the NAR teachings are not receiving the nutrition that their spirits need, and so they are in a perpetual state of hunger. They believe that this is a good hunger but, in fact, it's a sign that they have been poisoned. Their senses are stimulated and entertained, yet their spirits are starving. Their flesh is elevated instead of crucified.

Are you in any way involved in the New Apostolic Reformation? There is only one solution, and that is to **flee from this delusion that will shipwreck your faith**. Whether you are in full-time or part-time ministry, a volunteer, or simply a member, I implore you to search the Scriptures, and ask God to open your eyes to this deception. It's not good enough to say, "I'll pray about it and see if I have peace," or "I'll ask the Lord for direction and obey Him." Friend, God has already spoken and given direction—it's in his infallible Word.

All the teachings of the NAR can be clearly refuted with Scripture. These are not non-essentials that fellow believers can agree to disagree over.

But the things I have outlined are essential issues in clear contradiction of God's Word. **Any "peace" you feel while being a part of the New Apostolic Reformation is an emotion that is lying to you. It's a peace that comes from a deluded state.**

For believers coming out of the NAR, the transition from a feeling-based to a faith-based walk in Christ is but one of the incredible blessings when you leave this movement. What you believe you may have lost by leaving as far as friendships, time and money invested and reputation—**God is more than able to restore.**

> *We know that for those who love God all things work together for good, for those who are called according to his purpose.* Romans 8:28.

# IX. Conclusion

## Bob Brunette

We live in days that include a time of great apostasy—days in which very soon, genuine Christians will be persecuted—perhaps the most by the vast majority of so-called evangelical Christians. This group of evangelical Christians have settled for one of the numerous "other gospel" accounts such as: The New Apostolic Reformation (NAR), Word of Faith (WOF), and the Emergent Church, to name a few. There is also a whole host of false prophets and prosperity pimps who have licensed themselves a more convenient and suitable pseudo-gospel—a gospel that bodes well with "living your best life now," along with inheriting the kingdom of God philosophy. They peddle a Christian package that Satan himself would relish. It is a pseudo-gospel that has effectively removed the Cornerstone (of the genuine, glorious Gospel of Jesus Christ)—who happens to be the true head of the church. Furthermore, they have effectively eliminated the most fundamental requirements of what it means to become a genuine disciple of Christ in earnest!

> *And He was saying to them all, "If anyone wishes to come after Me, he must deny himself, and take up his cross daily and follow Me. For whoever wishes to save his life will lose it,*

*but whoever loses his life for My sake, he is the one who will save it.* Luke 9:23, 24

We are living in a time when the vast majority of present day American evangelical Christians would have us believe that American Evangelical Christianity (AEC) has become 100 miles wide when, in fact, it is but a mere inch in width. We can read in Revelation 3:17-18, the spiritual condition we see unfolding in the vast majority of AEC in a day when she is guilty of the very charge that the Lord brought against the church of Laodicea.

> *Because you say, "I am rich, and have become wealthy, and have need of nothing," and you do not know that you are wretched and miserable and poor and blind and naked, I advise you to buy from Me gold refined by fire so that you may become rich, and white garments so that you may clothe yourself, and that the shame of your nakedness will not be revealed; and eye salve to anoint your eyes so that you may see!*

Also, we are living in the very thick of a great falling away that may very well be the "Great Falling Away" that will usher in the Second Coming of Christ! In fact, it is difficult to find a church across America that preaches the uncompromised gospel of Christ.

It has been said the first time you hear the truth—it will sound like a lie! More often than not, it's been my personal experience in my Christian pilgrimage of 42 plus years, that when the Lord Jesus (the only one worthy of being called, "rabbi") reveals spiritual truths to us—it ends up turning our world upside down and inside out! Enough can't be said about the "stone which the builders rejected" that became the Cornerstone! Also, the Bible tells us in I Peter 2:4-8 that Jesus personally became a "Stone of Stumbling and a Rock of Offense" to those who are disobedient to the Word of God!

> *And coming to Him as to a living stone which has been rejected by men, but is choice and precious in the sight of God, you also, as living stones, are being built up as a spiritual house for a holy priesthood, to offer up spiritual sacrifices acceptable to God through Jesus Christ.* For this is contained in Scripture:

*"BEHOLD, I LAY IN ZION A CHOICE STONE, A PRECIOUS CORNER stone, and HE WHO BELIEVES IN HIM WILL NOT BE DISAPPOINTED."*

*This precious value, then, is for you who believe; but for those who disbelieve,*

*"THE STONE WHICH THE BUILDERS REJECTED, THIS BECAME THE VERY CORNER stone," and, "A STONE OF STUMBLING AND A ROCK OF OFFENSE";*

*for they stumble because they are disobedient to the Word, and to this doom they were also appointed!*

**WARNING**: We, as disciples of Christ, need to recognize some sobering truths with regard to Satan and his undertakings. In reality, he represents a very powerful spiritual foe, while simultaneously recognizing that he is a created being. And in that created state, he comes well-equipped with a vast arsenal of nuclear-like weaponry which he can draw upon, at will, in both the spiritual as well as the physical realms.

We would be remiss in not simultaneously pointing out that his assaults come embedded with thousands of years of experience at deceiving the souls of men. As followers of Christ, we must recognize that his most piercing and cutting assaults will come under a chameleon-like cover—in the form of a pseudo-Christian masquerade. He will not appear draped in a conspicuous red leotard-like outfit exhibiting pointed horns and a pointed tail while sporting a pitch fork—but rather as a prominent evangelical figure! This especially includes the host of NAR leaders we see flooding the spiritual landscape of present day American Evangelical Christianity. They appear postured as some of the most popular so-called Christian leaders while operating undercover as agents of hell.

As disciples of Christ, it behooves us to recognize that the Creator in His sovereign and absolute control of the entire universe, is not taken aback by a single scheme of the evil one. Recognizing that Satan, roaring lion though he may be, nonetheless, remains in his original state—that of a created being. He is essentially kept on a spiritual leash, where every single one of his undertakings is subject to the sovereign and absolute control of the one and only true God, namely the Creator of the universe.

137

Satan in his most pointed, inflamed assaults are unequivocally restricted to the absolute will of Almighty God being accomplished on earth even as it is in heaven!

> *The Lord has made everything for its own purpose, even the wicked or the day of evil!* Proverbs 16:4

> *The One forming light and creating darkness, causing well-being and creating calamity; I am the Lord who does all these!* Isaiah 45:7

We need to recognize that as genuine disciples of Christ, there are many, perhaps even most, within the greater NAR movement, who lack the very teeth of the real gospel message—the preaching of the cross!

> *Indeed we have the sentence of death within ourselves, so that we should not trust in ourselves, but in God who raises the dead!* II Corinthians 1:9

False prophets and their false teaching movements are entirely void of even the slightest measure of genuine inspiration whatsoever as to what it means to be a disciple of Jesus of Nazareth, who hung on a cross at Calvary.

> *For many walk, of whom I often told you, and now tell you even weeping, that they are enemies of the cross of Christ, whose end is destruction, whose god is their appetite, and whose glory is in their shame, who set their minds on earthly things!* Philippians 3:18-19

Let us not be so naïve to believe for a single moment that just because someone identifies themselves as an evangelical Christian, as their title would imply, that they are supremely and unequivocally submitted to the authority of Christ. But that they are rather more satisfied, more comfortable with a substitute "your best life now," a Joel Osteen-like gospel—with a Christ of their own making. They have no reservations, whatsoever, in calling their false god, "Jesus Christ," when in reality they have created for themselves a false god—"another Jesus"—an idol that they worship with great zeal. When compared against Holy Writ, by the power of the Holy Spirit, it can be quickly judged as heresy. The genuine Apostle Paul concurs in Galatians 1:6-9:

> *I am amazed that you are so quickly deserting Him who called you by the grace of Christ, for a different gospel; which is really not another; only there are some who are disturbing you and want to distort the gospel of Christ. But even if we, or an angel from heaven, should preach to you a gospel contrary to what we have preached to you, he is to be accursed! As we have said before, so I say again now, if any man is preaching to you a gospel contrary to what you received, he is to be accursed!*

At best, the NAR movement represents what we see the genuine prophets of God, Jeremiah and Isaiah, recognize taking place in their day—a whole host of false prophets coming to the fore!

> *For My people have committed two evils: They have forsaken Me, The fountain of living waters, To hew for themselves cisterns, Broken cisterns That can hold no water!* Jeremiah 2:13

> *Woe to the rebellious children," declares the Lord, Who execute a plan, but not Mine, And make an alliance, but not of My Spirit, In order to add sin to sin!* Isaiah 30:1

I would be grossly negligent in my witness for Christ in not conveying that false prophets are the judgment of God, destined to test the hearts of men, in striking contrast to what their outward appearance would have us believe about them.

> *For thus says the Lord of hosts, the God of Israel, 'Do not let your prophets who are in your midst and your diviners deceive you, and do not listen to the dreams which they dream. For they prophesy falsely to you in My Name; I have not sent them,' declares the Lord! "Woe to the shepherds who are destroying and scattering the sheep of My pasture!" declares the Lord. Therefore thus says the Lord God of Israel concerning the shepherds who are tending My people: "You have scattered My flock and driven them away, and have not*

*attended to them; behold, I am about to attend to you for the evil of your deeds," declares the Lord.* Jeremiah 23:1-2. (Please also see Jeremiah 29:8-9 and Jeremiah 23:11-32.)

+++++++

False prophets and occult practices invading the church are nothing new. The early church experienced them as well. When some of the Christian followers in the Book of Acts realized what they had been involved in were offensive to God, they humbled themselves, confessed their sins, and then burned their books publicly. It is obvious that they did not want a mixture, and they certainly did not try to justify their involvement with false practices. In fact, we see in Acts 19:17-20 that they did not see any value in them at all. On the contrary, they had one huge bonfire to destroy them. And as a result, the word of the Lord grew mightily.

> **This [the sons of Sceva] became known to all, both Jews and Greeks who lived in Ephesus: fear fell upon them all and the name of the Lord Jesus was being magnified. Many also of those who had believed kept coming, confessing and disclosing their practices. And many of those who practiced magic brought their books together and began burning them in the sight of everyone; and they counted up the price of them and found it fifty thousand pieces of silver. So the word of the Lord was growing mightily and prevailing.** Acts 19:17-20

We hope you will do your own research and take the matter as seriously as the early Christians did. Seek the Lord earnestly. If you find that you have strayed from the narrow path that leads to eternal life, and find yourself on a hidden path that leads to destruction by engaging in the practices of the New Apostolic Reformation, Bethel Church, the New Age or hyper-charismania/Kingdom Now belief systems as outlined in this book—join the thousands that are coming out of these movements. PLEASE REPENT for your involvement, and call on the Lord Jesus Christ and ask Him for forgiveness. He is faithful to forgive you and cleanse you from all unrighteousness. The Word of God will encourage and lead you into all truth.

Also, pray for the lost leaders and followers who are caught up in all forms of deception—that their eyes would be open and that they would humbly receive a true revelation of Jesus Christ and His truth.

We conclude with the words of two kings: one from King David in Psalm 24 and the other from King Jesus in Luke 12:37 along with a traditional hymn. To God be all the glory and honor and praise:

*The earth is the LORD's, and all it contains,*
*The world, and those who dwell in it.*
*For He has founded it upon the seas*
*And established it upon the rivers.*
*Who may ascend into the hill of the LORD?*
*And who may stand in His holy place?*
*He who has clean hands and a pure heart,*
*Who has not lifted up his soul to falsehood*
*And has not sworn deceitfully.*

*He shall receive a blessing from the LORD*
*And righteousness from the God of his salvation.*
*This is the generation of those who seek Him,*
*Who seek Your face—even Jacob      Selah.*
*Lift up your heads, O gates,*
*And be lifted up, O ancient doors,*
*That the King of glory may come in!*
*Who is the King of glory?*
*The LORD strong and mighty,*
*The LORD mighty in battle.*
*Lift up your heads, O gates,*
*And lift them up, O ancient doors,*
*That the King of glory may come in!*
*Who is this King of glory?*
*The LORD of hosts, He is the King of glory.      Selah.      Psalm 24*

*Blessed are those servants whom the Lord will find watching*
*when He comes.* Luke 12:37

Are you watching?

# THE CHURCH'S ONE FOUNDATION

Samuel John Stone -- 1866                    Samuel Sebastian Wesley – 1884

The church's one foundation is Jesus Christ her Lord.
She is His new creation by water and the word.
From heaven He came and sought her to be His holy bride.
With His own blood He bought her, and for her life He died.

Elect from every nation, yet one o'er all the earth,
her charter of salvation: one Lord, one faith, one birth.
One holy name she blesses, partakes one holy food.
and to one hope she presses, with every grace endued.

**Though with a scornful wonder this world sees her oppressed,**
**by schisms rent asunder, by heresies distressed,**
**yet saints their watch are keeping; their cry goes up: "How long?"**
**And soon the night of weeping, shall be the morning song.**

Mid toil and tribulation, and tumult of her war,
she waits the consummation of peace forevermore:
till with the vision glorious her longing eyes are blest,
and the great church victorious shall be the church at rest.

Made in the USA
Monee, IL
29 July 2022